"I have come to really [W9-CRD-561] *Dayle Maloney and his tremendous work ethic and care for people. Anyone who has come from where he has, and gone to where he has gone is an inspiration to us all."*

— Ed Foreman
Speaker, Businessman and
Former United States Congressman

"A tremendous book for all reasons and seasons. The great laws of success are presented with such warmth and simplicity that you forget you're reading a book.

The story behind every successful life is a hero, a mentor or a role model. In these pages you will find all three. No one can read this book without being encouraged and challenged, and you'll discover it is even better when you share it with others."

Read, Think, Share

— Charlie "Tremendous" Jones
International Speaker and Author

I Could Have Quit $7,000,000.00 Ago

Proof — Nice Guys Do Finish First!

How Dayle Maloney and friends climbed to success in network marketing as told to

Lori Prokop

RoseArt Publishing

All claims contained in this book are true, to the best of the author's and publisher's knowledge. In no case did the distributors included in this book imply to the author that their experiences or incomes were typical for their company or for the network marketing industry. Given the inherently risky nature of business, the author and publisher urge readers to conduct their own research before investing their time or their money. The publisher and author disclaim any warranty, expressed or implied, and shall have neither liability nor responsibility to any person or entity regarding the financial results from the use of the methods, advice, systems, or information contained in this book. Network Marketing is not a get-rich scheme. Anyone who decides to start a home-based business must expect to invest time, effort and capital. Some people find network marketing more lucrative than working for others. Every effort had been made to make this text as complete and accurate as possible. However, there may be mistakes both typographical and in content. Therefore, this text should only be used as a general guide and not as the ultimate source of network marketing information.

How to order:

Single and multiple copies may be ordered from: Dayle Maloney & Associates, Ltd., 3301 Golf Road, Eau Claire, Wisconsin, 54701 (800) 457-6588 or (800) 621-2065

To contact the author: Lori Prokop (800) OWN-BOSS, 800-696-2677 or 612-437-3132 or by e-mail at lprokop@isd.net

Contents

Contents

Contents

Chapter 5: Can't Is A Four Letter Word

Contents

Chapter 6: Can They Fog A Mirror?

Contents

Chapter 7: If You Aren't Plugged In — You Can't Get Turned On

Contents

Chapter 8: And Now For The Rest Of The Story...

Introduction

Author's Note: Newton "Newt" Kindlund is President and Chairman of the Board of Holiday RV Superstores, Inc., a recreational vehicle dealership comprised of nine locations throughout the United States, representing over 51 brands of recreational vehicles and boats. Mr. Kindlund teaches entrepreneurship at Rollins College in Florida. He earned the 1992 SBA Small Business Person of the Year Award, the 1995 Executive of the Year Award and was a finalist for the Florida Entrepreneur of the Year. Newt and his wife Joanne, co-founders of Holiday RV Superstores, Inc., have three children: Kirsten, Erika and Darien. All have gone on to successful careers.

Dayle Maloney has changed the course of thousands of people's lives for the better, including mine.

In 1964, we met as competing field managers for a small corporation in Michigan called the Vesely Company, manufacturers of the Apache Camping Trailers. Our jobs were to visit Apache dealerships and increase revenues by helping them sell more campers.

Dayle's dealerships sold circles around the rest of ours. I asked, "Dayle, what the heck are you doing out there?"

He clued me in, "Newt, I'm not in the business of selling tent trailers or recreational vehicles for these dealers. I'm in the business of training salespeople how to prospect and successfully close the vehicle purchase."

Everyone but Dayle was attempting to save those dealerships one camper at a time. Dayle was duplicating himself by teaching salespeople his 10-step sales system. It was a planned sequence of events from exactly how a salesperson approached a family to the family proudly hooking up their new camper and taking it home. Those RV dealers loved Dayle and so did their bankers.

We called Dayle Mr. Ideaman. He wrote promotional ad copy so strong that when we gave away free hotdogs-on-a-bun, people drove for miles for the experience. One family traveled over 250 miles to discover what a "Chuckwagon Tube Steak" really was. Dayle made buying a camper fun and the families loved him for it.

When he wasn't pitching tube steaks, he was cooking up countless contests to tickle the media. I remember the "Who Can Kiss a RV The Longest?" contest (customers would actually keep their *lips* on a RV for *hours*). The media fell in love with Dayle, and his antics were big news.

I remember Dayle standing on the roof of a camper beating it with a baseball bat, making a terrible racket, to demonstrate how resilient the sidewalls were. The media gathered in droves to report on this "man-gone-mad."

Through all his creativity, Dayle is capable of focusing and delivering on his never-ending ideas — like very few men I've known. He was instrumental in bringing promotions and events to the recreational vehicle trade, and his reputation in the industry is world renowned to this day. That's quite a credit to a man who left the RV industry 20 years ago. We miss Old Dayle Maloney and would like him back, but I don't think network marketing is ready to let go of him.

Two years ago, I had the pleasure of meeting one of Dayle's distributors. The experience was inspirational — unlike anything I had encountered before. Dayle had instilled in the young woman a sense of personal ownership in her Nutrition For Life business. She had an extraordinary belief and determination to succeed because she had a pledge, based on a handshake, from Dayle Maloney. In any industry only a few people like Dayle come along every decade or two.

When Dayle became involved in Nutrition For Life, he didn't possess any academic schooling in medicine or in health care. He learned his new trade and proceeded to attack the network marketing industry with the same vigor he unleashed in the recreation vehicle business.

As a teenager, Dayle had polio and it forged his remarkable determination to rise above handicaps and make situations work out for the best. He is truly a man of inspiration. He has earned my unending respect.

I remember in the early days, traveling to dealerships together. We would check into a hotel at midnight after a full day of selling campers and working with dealers. The first thing Dayle would do was draw a hot bath of water. I'd have to pull him out of the tub an hour and a half later, just to get him in bed. My heart ached to look into his eyes and witness the daily physical pain polio had left him with. But, without complaint, he'd keep pushing on.

Every morning Dayle would be the first to wake, the first with ideas, the first ready to go! Most people would be soaked in self pity, trying to explain to the world why they couldn't get out of bed, not to mention tackle the challenge of another day.

If anything exemplifies the real meaning of Dayle's success, it is brute determination. Dayle and I both have had roller coaster careers — great successes and great setbacks. We each decided we were bound and determined to succeed.

Through adverse times, we didn't jump ship, we didn't bail out. Along with our loved ones, we did whatever it took to succeed — sold homes, lost homes and made whatever sacrifices for the success of our businesses which we had to make.

The story which will unfold for you within these pages is an inspiration to entrepreneurs. I don't fathom current business school graduates, those with the vertical careers which resemble rocket ships, are capable of understanding and appreciating this work. From what I've seen, they live in a world of capitalists, super leverage and, "Hey, if it doesn't work, you bail. You sting your investors and move to something else."

Dayle, on the other hand, is a study of determination, perseverance, character, integrity and "staying the course." The entrepreneurial spirit in all of us is a flame which kindles brightly when a person like Dayle enters our universe. He inspires people to believe in their abilities to achieve their dreams. The reality for most people is that life is not a rocket ship to the moon. Rather, it is a series of roller coaster rides. Your perseverance and determination to achieve are the trademarks of your character.

Twenty years ago, my wife, Joanne and I started a little "mom and pop" recreational vehicle business. Today, our company, Holiday RV Superstores, Inc. is a $75 million dollar enterprise whose stock has been traded for 10 years on NASDAQ (symbol: RVEE).

Through all our success, I have only one regret. When Joanne and I were just starting, I offered Dayle a partnership in the business. He would handle sales, I would handle administration, and Joanne would handle finance. Dayle decided to move in a different direction.

Joanne and I have accomplished quite a bit in 20 years, but I believe had Dayle been our partner, we would have gone well *beyond* where we are today. My regret is that I let him off the hook too easily. I shouldn't have accepted "No" for an answer.

So to all the network marketers reading this book, Dayle and his heart are yours for the asking. Don't make the same mistake I did and let go of him. If you do, it will haunt you for the rest of your life. Be smart and hold on tight to my friend, Dayle Maloney. I know you will enjoy the ride.

Newton C. Kindlund

Newton "Newt" Kindlund is President and Chairman of the Board of Holiday RV Superstores, Inc.,

Author's Acknowledgements

Special thanks to Dayle Maloney who overcame insurmountable adversities leading others to believe their lives can be improved no matter what their plight. Thank you to the people who kindly gave precious time from their busy schedules to participate in this book by sharing their stories and pictures.

To my life love, Marty, my very patient husband, who always supports my excitement and drive to work with laser beam focus to complete my projects with excellence — even when it means you have to go fishing without me. Geri Prokop, Proof Reader and Transcriber Extraordinaire, whose support and unbending belief I greatly appreciate, who is always more than patient with my latest projects and the extreme work schedules they create.

My very talented Editor, Linda Cadwalader Gulbrandson, whose knowledge of the English language greatly enhanced this book. To her husband, Mark, who generously gave up time with Linda so we could meet our deadlines. Tad Stittsworth whose insight and interviews provided us with a rich glimpse of the people's lives portrayed in this book. Sue Caldwell who stayed at Tad's and my side to make sure the interviews were transcribed perfectly.

David Bertrand and Jana Mitcham. President and Executive Vice-President of Nutrition For Life for their vision and belief in the power of placing this story on paper. Tara and Tracy Ternberg, Connie, Donna and the staff of Dayle's office for doing whatever it took to make this book a reality.

To you, the network marketer, I thank you for the role you have played in developing this industry into the powerhouse it is today.

Chapter 1

My Obligation Is To Do The Right Thing — The Rest Is In God's Hands

---

PART 1

You Never Know If "Later" Will Ever Come

The 1997 Nutrition For Life National Convention in Minneapolis, Minnesota, was well underway. Thousands of extremely excited, successful men and women were in attendance. I was the afternoon speaker right after former First Lady, Barbara Bush.

From the stage it was a blanket of white shirts, ties,

suits and sparkling jewels. I poured every bit of myself into that crowd, and they responded with roars of loving appreciation, lifting the roof of the convention center several feet. At times, the echoes in my ears were so intense, I wasn't sure if I was talking or just thinking about what I wanted to say next. We — all 5,000 of us — felt elated to be in each other's company.

As the Saturday afternoon session came to an end, the crowd began to clear out for the break between sessions. I was working my way to the exit door, feeling a little tired, as I had given my all on stage. I needed to rush back to my room, change from my suit into formal evening attire and get to the next event. My mind was preoccupied with the tuxedo I was going to be momentarily wrestling. Hard to believe at sixty-two years of age it was the first time I would wear a tux. I had no idea what to expect.

I was almost to the exit when two couples approached me and asked, "Do you suppose there is any chance we can stop you for a picture with each of us?"

"Hey, you better believe you can. Where are you all from?" I asked as I lined up with my arms around one of the couples.

They said, "Joplin, Missouri. When are you going to come to Joplin?"

I travel 200,000 miles a year giving speeches. I smiled, "Whenever you need me, just call. I'll come to Joplin, Missouri."

After the photos, I rushed off to my hotel room to deal with that tuxedo and make my appearance for the early-evening formal dinner event.

Later that Saturday night, after the formal dinner event, thousands of people gathered in the auditorium for the evening session. Dale Brunner was speaking on stage. Emotions were high as recognition was being given to those who'd worked all year for this moment.

Without warning, tragedy struck. Thousands watched motionless as a faint voice cried out for help, permeating the ocean of people. Confusion silenced the crowd. Doctors and nurses rushed to the side of a man who suffered a sudden, heart attack. We stood in disbelief. We prayed. We hoped. We witnessed how fragile life really is. The prayers of a crowd of 5,000 people couldn't save that life. The man died the following Tuesday.

I was told he was Dale Hedgcorth from Joplin, Missouri. For a long time, I wondered if I had met him when those two couples stopped me on the way out of the convention hall. I often thought, "Did I ever meet Dale Hedgcorth?"

A few months later in November, 1997, I was in San Diego, and a man and his wife came up to me and said, "We're so happy you're coming to Joplin, Missouri on January 30."

"Yeah, I'm looking forward to it, too. I just can't wait to get there," I smiled as anticipation filled my heart.

They said, "Well, we'll tell you *who* is really looking forward to it — Dale Hedgcorth's widow, Katherine."

My heart paused with a silent ache.

Now, I can't see very well — I'm blind in one eye and

can't see much out of the other, but I strained to take a real good look. The couple introduced themselves. To my joy, I was speaking to Dale Hedgcorth's brother-in-law, Bob, and sister, Fran Heiniger. They said, "Boy, is Dale's wife waiting to see you. She has this big picture of you with Dale just about four hours before he had the heart attack. You can't believe how happy you made that man. He couldn't believe he could watch you up on stage with thousands of people cheering for you, and you would stop and have your picture taken with us."

January, 1998, when I arrived in Joplin, Missouri, I spoke with Dale's brother-in-law and a group of other people about the tragedy in Minneapolis. His heart-touching story reminded us all of how precious and short life really is. I met Dale's wife, Katherine, at the back of the room. She was embracing an 8½ by 11 colored picture and handed it to me. I pulled the photograph close to my left eye and took a real strong, deep look into that picture. There was the man of the moment, who was in all of our hearts, Dale Hedgcorth. My eyes swelled with tears as his wife asked me to sign the picture telling me it was one of her most prized possessions.

I had met Dale for the first time — the only time — four hours before he had the heart attack which took his life. I didn't know at the time the impact our brief meeting would have on all of our lives. Chances are — if you were in my shoes, you wouldn't have either.

The truth is when Dale asked me for the picture, I was thinking of myself and my problems. I could have easily said, "Hey, I'm in a hurry. I gotta get back to my room. I've gotta get into a tuxedo for the first time in my life. I need to go to the big dinner event. Maybe a little later, huh?"

Later may never come.

I am so happy I stopped and had that picture taken! Never turn anybody down. *Never*.

Did I stop because I really like having my picture taken? Anyone who knows me realizes I'm not highly photogenic — to put it mildly. In fact, for the cover of this book, we took about 400 photos to get one that even looked decent.

It's not about photos at all. It's about giving of your time, love and consideration to others. In the midst of everyday living, there are no bells or whistles that go off when you touch a person's life. Usually, it goes unannounced. Sometimes you don't realize a thing. Other times you feel it in your heart. All I knew at the time was those people from Joplin were real happy that Saturday afternoon in 1997.

After meeting Bob and Fran Heiniger the morning of the Trudeau Family Reunion in San Diego in November, 1997 — a few months after Dale Hedgcorth passed on and prior to my visit to Joplin — I was rushing through the lobby of the hotel at a pretty good clip for an old guy who can't walk very well. (Polio took my walking strength about 45 years ago.) A woman asked me to stop for a moment so she could have her picture taken with me. I was on my way to a meeting thinking about myself, confused and having a problem figuring out the hotel. I was already seven minutes late and the meeting was only 30 minutes long.

I said, "Listen, can it wait until just a little later? Can you catch me then? I'm really late for this meeting and I'm real sorry, but I just can't do it." Instantly, my own words crushed my heart. How could I have turned her down?

She and I didn't meet up that evening and it haunted

me all night long. That night I must have awakened about 50 times. I couldn't sleep. My heart wouldn't let me forget Dale Hedgcorth and the choice I had made with the woman in the lobby.

The next day, when it was my turn to go on stage, I opened my speech with an apology deep from within my heart. I told our Nutrition for Life Four-Star and Five-Star Platinum leaders, "Don't ever turn down anybody for a photo. Let them use your credibility. Give them that picture so they can take it back to their families and friends."

Then I continued: "There was a woman who asked me last night for a picture. I turned you down. It was wrong ... very wrong, and it's bothered me all night long. If you haven't got that picture and you'd still like one, see me afterwards. I'll be back at the table and you can have all the pictures you want."

I was on my way back to the table and the woman stopped me with a big hug saying, "I still haven't got the picture and I'd like one." I smiled; with relief. I just can't stand to turn people down.

It was Dale Hedgcorth's brother-in law, Bob, who that very weekend reminded me of the importance of being there for the people. When this woman approached me, and I turned her down for the picture she wanted, I couldn't forgive myself. Thank goodness for the lesson Dale Hedgcorth taught me several months earlier, and thank God I listened. How do you imagine I would have felt if I had flunked the lesson the first time it came around with Dale at the National Convention?

With each decision you make, please let your heart remind you ... later may never come.

Success Secret ...

"Remember that every single person you or I talk to is the most important person we've talked to all day."

Dale Hedgcorth, Dayle Maloney, Katherine Hedgcorth
Nutrition For Life National Convention,
Minneapolis, Minnesota August 30, 1997

This book is dedicated in loving memory of Dale Hedgcorth

PART 2

Saddle Your Dreams Before You Ride Them

I did not build my success alone. With the help of others, I can assure you that nice guys and gals do finish first. Even though I can boast the income of a multi-millionaire, what's more important is the feeling I have of total security. It has nothing to do with money; it's about friendships.

Some people may say, "Sure, Dayle, that's easy for you to say. You've already got the money!" Well, if you've got a few minutes, join me here in my office. Why don't you pull up that chair? Yes, that one over there. It's the best one in the house, far better than this rickety old one I've grown to like. Pull it up to the desk over here. We'll keep each other company and let that sun shining through the bay window warm us. Let's relax and enjoy. Ahhhh, feels kind of good, doesn't it?

Hmmmm... Now, it hasn't always felt this good. Just 16 short years ago, my life was full of pain. I was financially broke. Had I been able to afford even a modest life insurance policy, I would have been worth more dead than alive. In those years, every moment of my life was made up of a mountain of pressure in trying to repay $350,000 in debt from credit cards, overdraft checks, investments gone bad, more bills than Carter had liver pills. My credit report read like a rap sheet: debts due immediately. The pressure was on.

I found myself in trouble and, for a period of time, had no straw to hold onto. I had made decisions that resulted in failures again and again. Mentally, the battle was bloody. How could I face my family and friends? I was failing in every way — fast.

As I felt the final cards of my life being dealt out of my control, my mind was covered by a heavy, dark blanket of doubt. I found a tiny, golden thread of hope as I was gasping for an answer. Like a breath of fresh air it came to me. It's here in this book — you have it in your hands. When you're finished you will have the instructions for a safety blanket of wealth. You will hear all, see all and learn all the moves I made to go from the darkest point in my life to being fortunate, wealthy and befriended by thousands. I don't tell you that to impress you, but rather to impress *upon you* what is real, possible and available to you, too.

This book is full of stories — a fair sprinkling of mine and those which come from friends. Most everyone who has been so kind to share his or her story was an underdog at one time. You'll hear from nice people who have made it big on their own terms.

This book is full of people who some might call "big shooters" — but they are *not*. They are little shooters who just kept shooting. They have captured and live the American Dream. Within these pages, you'll see how you can do the same.

What do you need to succeed? Let's first talk about

what doesn't matter:

Your present situation? Doesn't matter how good or bad.

Your past? Doesn't matter where you've been. I won't ask unless you want me to listen.

Where you grew up? Irrelevant. I grew up on the wrong-side-of-the-tracks, so poor that the poor folks thought I was poor.

What you have or don't have? None of that matters.

Who you know or don't know? Unimportant. You'll soon find yourself with more friends and substantial relationships than you know what to do with.

What matters this moment is where you want to go, that you have a dream to point you in the right direction. I believe in you and will help you find your dream, if need be. The secrets discovered on the pages you are holding in your hands right now will help you get there. So c'mon my friend. Let's get started.

Success Secret...

"Faith is daring the soul to go
beyond what the eyes can see."

Chapter 2

Triumph Is Just "Umph" Added To Try

PART 1

Don't Judge My Future Destination By My Present Location

People search for that magical something that makes us complete. We choose goals and change goals. We dance to a melody of hope and heartbreak all the while wondering if there is something more perfect to be lived right now.

If you are reading this book you might be trying to decide if life is worth the effort. Maybe life hasn't dealt you a fair hand.

Promise me one thing. Invest your time to read this book.

Remember, I won't ask where you've been. What I care about is you *today* and where you want to go. I don't care to see a resume; I care if you have a dream. I grew up on the wrong-side-of-the-tracks, but I wouldn't let the wrong side of the tracks grow up in me! You have nothing to do with your beginning and everything to do with your ending.

If you don't have a dream, if life's gotten so rough that you have lost it or you never learned how to dream, I'll teach you. When you come right down to it, a dream is the hope that keeps us alive in a world that sometimes isn't worth a hill of beans.

So wherever you are in life, content or not, promise me right now you'll read this book from cover to cover. It will show you exactly how to make it: how to dream and how to achieve. I care what *your* dream is. My dream is to help you realize your dream. So, how about it, do we have a deal? You keep on reading and I'll be here with you every step of the way. There are ten success ingredients you'll need on your journey: number one is a dream; number two is a dream; number three is a dream; number four, five, six, seven, eight, nine and ten are all a DREAM!

Since we're doing this together, I've got to ask you to bear with me. I'm not a professional writer. You're not going to hear from a guy who's got all the right words and all the correct English. No, that's not me. You're going to hear from a guy who's coming straight from the heart because I believe in you. I believe in network marketing. I believe in Nutrition For Life. I believe in the *American Dream*. I believe you can go all the way to the top. And if you want, we'll do it together. You've now just started a journey to your destination.

Some might think these are some lofty promises

coming from an average guy. The thought may cross some folk's minds, "Dayle, what makes you think you're smart enough to have something like success all figured out?"

Oh, I wouldn't say it's smarts — at least not the book learning kind. I don't have a college degree. What I do is follow the PC Rule: "persistency and consistency." Persistence makes all the difference in the world. When people tell you that you don't have what it takes to do something, you tell them to get out of the way because you're going to do it!

But all the desire and persistence in the world is only half-baked if you don't have the right business vehicle to achieve what you want. I'll show you what I mean. I'll share my background to show you there isn't anyone who can't succeed in this business.

I didn't have it easy in school or growing up. We lived in St. Croix Falls, Wisconsin, a quiet little town nestled on the banks of the St. Croix River. Up behind our house was a run-down, one-room shack an old bachelor lived in. About the same time my parents, my brother Mick, and I moved into our house, that bachelor went into a nursing home. His old place became part of my stomping grounds.

My mother was always sick in bed. First, she had ulcers. Then my mother had stomach cancer. I watched her die a terribly painful death. On her death bed I made her a promise that some day I'd make her proud of my accomplishments. I think she's proud of what I'm doing, but the pages of this book will let you be the judge of that.

My dad drank a lot. When it came to discipline, my father was judge, jury ... but mostly executioner.

To find some safety, some peace, I used to walk up
the back hill to the old shack. It's where I learned to dream.
That old place meant a lot to me. I'd like to take you there.
Thinking back — the shack was so dumpy, it almost
embarrasses me. But I know you're a friend. What do you
think? Have you got a minute? Awww, great, let's go.

Watch your step there getting out of the car. C'mon,
up the back hill over here. It's not too steep, but watch your
step just in case. See it over there? The old shack's about 50
feet from where we are now. I walk slowly since that polio
but we'll get there. It feels good to stretch the legs, huh?
That grass sure is green, but sometimes it can be slippery, so
take good care. It's a little jaunt, huh? A few more feet and,
well, here it is ... the old wooden shack. It is amazing there is
anything left. Back then it was the dumpiest thing around,
even rougher than the old house where I grew up.

Just take a look at the walls of this shack. They surely
have warped through the years, and the sun has bleached the
wood almost white. Yeah, it leaked water like a sieve back
then, too. Watch your step. Hear those floor boards creak?
Be careful and step lightly on only the boards that look all
there. If you see one splintered — like that one to your right
— step around it.

I've got something to show you. There, over to the
left, in the corner. See that wooden box with a hole in the
top? That was the bathroom. See the daylight shining up
through it? That hole goes directly to the ground. Hard to
believe we lived like that, huh?

Don't lean on the walls too hard; they look pretty
weak. Take a whiff of that old, musty mildew. That smell is
the same as I remember 50 years ago. It's still so strong you
can practically taste it in the air, can't you?

Now, the roof was all intact back then, but as you can see it's pretty much gone now. The bees' nest over there in the corner wasn't here back then. Don't worry, they're honeybees, and if we stay over here, they'll leave us alone. That buzzing won't hurt anything.

When I was 16 years old, I'd go trapping north of town on my bicycle to make some money. I'd skin my furs right over here. Well, I'll be danged! Look at this. One of the old knives I used on my furs. The old bachelor left it years ago. I used it but never took it out of here. It was the only sharp knife I had for the longest time. Here, feel that edge? Dull — a little rusty and rough, isn't it? Wonder if it could be sharpened up for old time's sake? Hmmm. I'll leave it here on the floor for nostalgia.

Look at this place. This is where I'd come to sit by the hour and dream. You can see there's no source of heat in this old shack. So in the wintertime, I'd hoof it up here in a heavy winter coat. I'd sit on an old wooden chair shivering for hours from the sharp, stinging cold — right here in the middle of the room — dreaming.

It was in this decrepit, little, old shack where I first learned how to use my imagination. Use your eyes and you can see there isn't anything to look at now. It wasn't any better back then. I guess having nothing to look at forced me to look inside my own mind.

What would I dream? I came up here when I first started trapping. I wanted to learn to be a good trapper. I didn't have any training and no one to teach me, so I'd dream about how to do it right. I'd read *Fur-Fish-and Game Magazine*. I eventually became good. I wanted forever to learn how to catch a mink because they said they were hard to catch. At

15, I sat right here and dreamed of catching a mink. Trapping got real hard after I had polio at 18. I couldn't get out in the water or in to the real muddy areas. When I was about 20, I caught my first mink. Two years later in the fall, I caught 69 mink checking the trap lines on my walking sticks. If I hadn't had polio, I would have trapped my whole life.

Later on, when my sight went because of bad retinas, I couldn't see much of what was around me. That served me well because I was left to look within my own mind, to my dreams.

The house in St. Croix Falls where I grew up.

Success Secret ...

> "I may not have much sight, but
> I feel sorry for people who have
> good sight but no vision."

"Here is the old shack ... how was your vision?"

Some people say they can't dream anymore. If you could feel, smell, hear, taste or use any of your senses to imagine this old shack, then you know how to dream. Dreaming or having a vision is first living life in the mind.

PART 2

Good Words Are Worth Much And Cost Little

I'm probably babbling. I don't even know if this interests you. Well, let's make it back down the hill. Thanks, friend, for coming up to see the old shack with me. That fresh air made me a little hungry. How about you? What if you and I go get a little something for the palate? I've got a few more things you might want to know.

When I was in 5th grade the Crosby Donkey Basketball Company came to town. It was a big-time fundraising event that excited our whole town where the merchants played the coaches.

Ten donkeys were trained to run the basketball court with players on their backs. Five players were on each team. The teachers selected 10 kids out of the 5th and 6th grades who each got to lead a donkey into the gymnasium the night of the game. Lo and behold, I was one of the 10 kids selected!

I had a grandmother who really helped me — my mother's mother — who I loved. She had a lot to do with my upbringing. I spent as much time as I could at her home on the lake in Frederic, Wisconsin. I always had good times at Granny's. When I was selected as one of the donkey kids, I called Granny gasping and squealing, "Granny, you got to get down here because I'm going to lead in a donkey!" Oh, man, I was *so excited.*

Granny made the run 25 miles from Frederic down to St. Croix Falls. The 10 kids, including me, had to be out there to meet the donkey guy at 6 o'clock that night. I'll never forget it. We were all uncontrollably chattering, like excited kids do.

Our chattering was muffled by the donkey guy's voice as he announced, "I'm looking for somebody here who wants to earn 50 cents tonight, two quarters. All you got to do is — you won't get to lead in a donkey — but you will have a broom and a dustpan and if any of these donkeys do a job out there, you run out there and clean it up right away. Sometimes you don't go out all night, but somebody is going to earn 50 cents."

I couldn't believe I heard him straight. My arm shot up like a bullet as I said, "I volunteer. Yes, sir." Boy, I needed the money. It *was two quarters.*

My poor grandmother. She was there so proud because she was waiting for her grandson to lead in a donkey. From off in the corner where I stood, I could see her straining her neck, looking and looking. To her disappointment and mine, I wasn't one of the 10.

But pretty soon, I made my grand entrance with my little broom and my little shovel and my dust pan. The entire place just let loose. It had to be the biggest roar all night. There was one donkey, Sassafras. I think he dumped four times that night.

The audience would just hoot and holler at me, but out I'd go. No matter how embarrassing, I never reneged on my job. I went out there *every time* and did the best I could — no matter how much they made fun of me or razzed me. I imagined the hard time I'd get from the kids in school the next day.

My dad was there, and after the show he shamed me: "You damn fool." It cut my heart like a knife. Even at 11 years old, there were times it was easier taking a right hook than hearing his sharp tones. At least flesh heals. But the heart feels forever.

My grandmother was proud of me. She stood by my side and wrapped an arm around me boasting, "Dayle, you did a good job." I loved my Granny.

The donkey guy broke through the crowd and walked up to Granny and me. My heart stopped. I didn't get those two quarters he promised me. He patted me on the back and said in front of everyone, "You did a great job, son." And he gave me *four quarters*! I had worked hard.

That made me feel real good, in spite of the razzing I knew I was going to get from the kids at school, and what I was sure my dad had in store for me once we got home.

Success Secret ...

"Speak kind words, and you will hear kind echoes."

PART 3

Don't Ever Let Your Problems Become Excuses

I graduated from high school and turned 18 in June, 1953. My grandmother wanted me to go to college so badly, it would bring tears to her eyes when she spoke about it. I wanted to go something fierce. Only one problem: I didn't have two nickels to rub together let alone enough money to make it to college. All summer I promised my grandmother when fall came she'd see me in college. I didn't know how, but I just couldn't let her down.

The nearer school time came, the more depressed and worried I got. My grandmother was the only one who believed in me. I loved her so much. The pressure in my heart grew like an over-inflated balloon as college classes were starting in just a few weeks and I hadn't even enrolled. How would I possibly tell her I wasn't going to make it to college that fall?

As fall of 1953 approached, America found itself in one of its last major polio epidemics. Call it guilt, coincidence, or escaping what I couldn't bear to deal with, but a month before college, I was diagnosed with a bad case of polio. The epidemic was so bad, they had no room in the special polio hospitals. I fought the polio at home for 3 weeks before they could get me into the Sheltering Arms Hospital, a part of the Sister Kenny Institute in Minneapolis.

When I was in the hospital with polio, I did the best I could do to get out of there. I fought hard, real hard. I knew in my heart I could lick it. I've always believed "when the going gets tough, the tough get going." In later years, Dr. Robert Schuller wrote a book called <u>Tough Times Don't Last But Tough People Do</u>. The title of that book sums up one of the main ingredients of success: persistence.

I felt real bad for the little, tiny kids — one or two years old. They would never know what it was to walk or run. I was 18 and I had that experience. It used to really bother me. I watched children die. It was tough.

I had a therapist, Teresa Lane. I hope she's reading this. Boy, she believed in me. I went through a therapy I called "treatments." They were very painful. I'd have hot packs so hot my muscles would smolder like lava from a volcano. I'd have soaks in water so scorching my skin would near blister. I wanted out of the hospital, so I'd take extra soaks and plead for extra hot packs.

A rope was tied to the foot of my bed. The nurses said the only way for me to get out of that hospital was if I could bend enough to place my forehead on my knees. With polio it was near impossible to do. My leg muscles felt as though they had shrunk like pieces of thin clear plastic over a fire. I painstakingly worked every waking hour grabbing that rope to pull my head to my knees.

About this time things were looking pretty grim. Then one day the doctor came into my room. It seemed his heart had hardened from the pain and suffering that surrounded him. He looked briefly at my chart, then at me, then his eyes moved downward as he spoke into my chart and said firmly, "Son, you'll probably *never* walk again. Get used to it!" He instructed the nurses, "The best you can do is continue the patient's therapy in attempt to stretch the leg muscles enough to straighten those legs. They might straighten up enough for braces, but they'll never be strong enough to bear any weight." Then he walked away. Shock filled my mind. Eighteen years old and never walk again? Angry hot tears streamed down my face.

The doctor did me a favor when he told me that. It made me work all the harder. When I look back at what had happened, God was making a better person out of me. I didn't think about it at the time, but I've thought about it many times afterwards. Everything wrong that has happened has been for the good. It's made me a stronger person.

Success Secret ...

"You can't plow a field by turning it over in your head. You have to work hard, but don't worry. You won't drown in your own sweat."

PART 4

Desires Determine Your Thoughts — Thoughts Determine Your Life

Each night before my therapist, Teresa, left the hospital she would come in and give me more "treatments." It was after her scheduled work day, and she didn't get paid a bit to do it. On Saturday and Sunday, her days off, she would come into the hospital to give me "treatments". Teresa had a good heart. She was never paid any extra money.

We worked hard and diligently as I was fighting the battle of my life, wanting to walk out of that hospital real bad. It took a long time before I took my first step alone with the walking sticks.

Success Secret ...

> "A great pleasure in life comes
> from doing what other people
> say is impossible."

At first, I didn't walk very well with the walking sticks. You've probably seen them. Each arm slides through a ring and my hands rested on a stump of a handle. I hated those sticks. When I'd go down the steps, I'd put the sticks on the step ahead of me and then move my legs down.

Well, one day I'm out with my buddies. Of course they're saying, "C'mon, let's go." So I try to take three or four steps at one time. All I did was pole vault myself. I broke the knee cap on my left leg which was my good leg. I didn't have enough strength in my right leg to move around. My heart sank. I couldn't believe it. I was laid up in the hospital again. That's about the closest I ever came to quitting for good. In fact, I did quit ... for about three hours.

After I could walk again, I was hired as the western Wisconsin correspondent for the *St. Paul Pioneer Press*. I wrote feature stories for a column called "A Line Of Baloney By Dayle Maloney" for the Sunday Wisconsin edition of the paper.

One morning, the front-page headline read "Tragedy Took The Lives Of 6 Local Teenagers In Head-on Crash With Bridge." Seven kids from River Falls, Wisconsin, had gone to the neighboring town of Spring Valley, Wisconsin, for the football game. It was reported they were drinking by the time they got to the game. On the way back home, they hit a bridge head-on. Six of the seven were killed.

The second day's story was the human interest side. I was quite good at that, so they sent me out to River Falls to try to find the "story behind the story." Once in River Falls I found an A&W Rootbeer Drive-in. I whipped in to get a burger and tried to figure how I was going to get that scoop. I could see a group of kids off to my left huddled around a picnic table. A couple of the girls were sobbing. I walked over and asked, "Hey, what's going on?" They told me mournfully, "Our friends were killed last night in a car accident." They talked. I listened.

Geez ... those kids took me all over. I think it helped both of us. Maybe it was just the therapy they needed. I was escorted to the home of one of the victims and met his parents. They showed me the clothes — the bloody clothes — he'd been wearing.

I remember when I went out to look at the scene of the crash and the car, there were beer cans scattered everywhere. Never once in the article did I mention alcohol was involved. I just couldn't do that to the parents, family, friends and people in that community. I was reprimanded by the editor because I didn't bring out the ugly side of the story. I just couldn't. That's one reason why I probably never stayed a reporter. I just couldn't stand to write bad about people. I still won't say bad things about people today.

The town folks told me that a couple nights a week you'd see this group of friends sitting at the corner booth at the Walvern Hotel in River Falls. To this day I remember how the first sentence of that story read in the morning paper: "There will be an empty booth in the Walvern Hotel tonight."

I found satisfaction in being a newspaper reporter, but I still wanted to be a big-time sports columnist or a coach. I loved sports but I wasn't really a good athlete, and the polio meant the end of my playing days.   So I organized and coached the city team. Back then, when you were out of high school sports, you could move on to the city team. I coached the softball and basketball teams. How did we do? Mostly, we just had fun. I wasn't a Vince Lombardi or Mike Holmgren.

That gave me the taste of coaching I was praying for. I decided coaching was what I really, really, really wanted to do with my life. I wanted to help people become their best. I prayed someday I could get enough money to go to college and become the coach for a major team. I dreamed everyday of being a coach. Funny thing is back then I thought I'd have to find the money first and the only kind of team a person could coach was comprised of professional athletes.

In 1985 I became an NFLI coach. I finally had my own team. Which team? The most powerful, professional team in the ranks: Nutrition For Life International — NFLI for short.

My prayers were answered. All those nights on bent knees pleading, "God, let me be an NFL coach" and all those times I closed my eyes and dreamed of an NFL team paid off. I am fortunate to be the personal business coach for thousands of NFLI business owners on how to take control of their time, reach their financial goals, feel alive again and win the game of life. I teach them there is light at the end of the tunnel, and it isn't a train.

I coach people. I give them hope during what are sometimes desperate situations. I've always been thankful for the coaching position life has entrusted me with. Remember when I thought I would need to find the money first and the coaching would follow? What happened in reality was I started coaching the people first and the money followed. Today, I coach 50,000 professional business people, many who endure with twice the fortitude of most athletes. I touch more lives, help more people one-on-one than I could have in any other coaching capacity.

Success Secret ...

> "The greatest achievements during your life are those which benefit other people."

Chapter 3

Hard Work Is The Yeast That Raises The $$Dough$$

PART 1

Our Destiny Changes With Our Thoughts

Few people succeed because they are *destined* to; *most* succeed because they are *determined* to. When you get right down to the root of the meaning of the word "succeed," you find it simply means to *follow through*.

I'd like to start introducing a few of the many thousands of people who have found success in their lives with network marketing and specifically Nutrition For Life. I've selected people from a variety of backgrounds hoping you will be able to relate to the situations of one or two of these folks. Each chapter from this point forward will be segmented into parts. Each part will indicate it contains an

interview from one of our distributors, or if it doesn't
introduce a distributor, it will contain a story I want to share
with you. To make it most enjoyable for you, each part will be
summed up with a Success Secret.

Although I have many, many close friends now, it was
very difficult for me when my grandmother died. She was my
sounding board — and, at that time, my only close, close
friend.

I've spent most of my adult life searching for that
magical something, striving to get my hands around the
feeling of being whole — of being a complete person. Today
there are three pools of love that I draw from to experience
that feeling: my beautiful wife, Jeannine; my deep-rooted
spiritual beliefs; and my many, many friends including the
100,000-plus people in Nutrition For Life.

I'm going to open the doors for you to two of my
pools: the relationship with my wife and the relationships with
friends and my Nutrition For Life organization.

My wife, Jeannine, and I were married in a little
ceremony at my home in White Bear Lake, Minnesota in
1972.   Just a few family members were there with us.
Nothing fancy, it's all we could afford. We were in our mid-
30's. That day, my mother-in-law took me aside, looked me
square in the eyes and said, "Dayle, you promise me that
you'll do whatever it takes to be a good husband and provider
for Jeannine." A lump swelled in my throat — only *I* knew we
were starting our life together $200,000 in debt. I hadn't even
told Jeannine. I looked at my mother-in-law and replied, "I
will."

Jeannine always believed in me. She has been the best partner for me in marriage and business that I could ever imagine. When times were hard, she was always generous with her patience. Rather than describing more about my relationship with Jeannine, I've asked the author, Lori Prokop, to interview my wife. Part Two of this chapter contains Lori's recent interview with Jeannine.

Success Secret ...

> "There are many things in life that will catch your eye, but only a few will catch your heart ... pursue those."

PART 2

A Happy Family
Is An Early Heaven

Jeannine Maloney
Life With Dayle

I'm a quiet person. My husband, Dayle, does enough talking for both of us; he's so good at it. He loves this business so much that he'll never slow down. I love Dayle very much. If I had to describe my husband, I would say he is the kindest man in the world. It amazes me how gentle-hearted he is. (Tears swell in her eyes as she reaches for a tissue.) I know some people see Dayle's kindness as a weakness. It's not.

How many people do you know that have thousands of friends who would come to their side if need be? Dayle has that because he's been so very kind and good to everybody he meets. We have a life of security knowing people will be there for us if we ever need it — just like Dayle and I have been there for them. That's *not* why we are so generous. It is simply part of what comes back from being good to people.

I'm a fairly reserved person. I don't take to people right away, but I do think the world of Nutrition For Life's President David Bertrand, and Executive Vice-President Jana Mitcham. They have been very good to us and Dayle's people. David and Jana have always made us feel a part of their family.

I love this business. It has allowed us to help a lot of people: our family, children in need, our community, distributors in the company and our church.

We have things I never thought we would have. We drive nice cars and have a very nice house. It took some getting used to. See, Dayle and I choose to live rather modestly. Our family and friends talked us into buying the house on the lake; otherwise, Dayle and I would have just lived in a little condo.

Nutrition For Life has a free car bonus program and we each have a Lexus. I'm very thankful — but a Lexus? My word. It took me a while to agree to drive a Lexus. Dayle and I are just not the big-shot types. Dayle always says he is just a little shot who keeps on shooting. When Dayle brought home the Lexus, I refused to drive it. Our pastor came over to the house and said, "Jeannine, you and Dayle earned it. Drive it." I agreed as long as I had the support of my friends and family. People who know me know it's a little much for my tastes. Nutrition For Life offers a free car program to all the distributors who qualify, and we're thankful for that. Hundreds of people in Dayle's organization have their monthly car payments made by David and Jana at Nutrition For Life. That takes a huge burden off people's shoulders and frees up the families' money.

What is most important to Dayle and me — what drives Dayle to keep going — is how many people we can help with the success and money. *Helping people* — that's what's exciting for both of us.

I don't think too many people know how Dayle and I ever got together.

We met when I worked for the district attorney in Grantsburg, Wisconsin. At the time, he was a writer for the *St. Paul Pioneer Press* and in the photography business with a friend. There was a murder, and Dayle and his partner had taken the pictures and written the story for the paper.

Dayle came into the district attorney's office with the pictures.

It was not love at first meeting for me because I thought I would always be single and had adjusted to that idea. I was not looking for a mate. I liked the independence of single life. We dated each other for 11 years — on and off. It was more *off* than it was *on* because Dayle was so busy. I can't remember what he did for a living for sure back then because he did so many things. He was always gone here and there. Most of our time together was on the phone. Dayle would call and we'd talk. We did not see each other very much at all.

When we did date, Dayle would pick me up and we'd go to Minneapolis for Chinese food. I would go shopping while Dayle went and did something else. He would pick me up from the mall at a certain time and we would drive back to Grantsburg, where I lived.

With Dayle's busy schedule, what do we do together *now*? We always have a project going that will help people, sometimes through our church and many other ways. Our favorite pastime together is eating. Isn't that something? Who else would admit it? But it's true. We love Chinese food. Wherever we travel, we are always on the lookout for the best Chinese restaurants. My favorite dish is Vegetable Lo Mein and Sweet and Sour Chicken. Dayle likes Egg Fu Yong and Fried Rice.

The other night Dayle and I were out to eat with friends, and they asked me where I grew up. I was born in Duluth. My mother was very sick while she was carrying me. The doctor in Frederic, Wisconsin told her to have an abortion because she and the baby would not live through the delivery, even though abortions were illegal.

My parents went to Duluth to live. That's where my mother's parents lived. My mother went to a doctor in Duluth where I was born.

I grew up in Branstad, Wisconsin, a teeny, tiny little town where one road went through the middle of town and there was a row of a few houses on each side. It was 3 miles from Grantsburg. Branstad was named for the main farmer in the area.

My father had a grocery store in Branstad and one in another little town nearby. My two sisters, Kathy and Marcia, and I had a really good life with a loving family and parents. My parents worked *hard*. The store was right next to our house. My sisters and I spent a great deal of time with my parents. Even though my parents worked from morning to night, my sisters and I still saw them a lot. That made a huge difference in our lives.

Tracy & Tara Ternberg and Jeannine & Dayle Maloney
Tracy & Tara are Jeannine & Dayle's
nephew-in-law and niece

Success Secret ...

> "If there is anything better
> than to be loved ...
> it is to love."

PART 3

It's Better To Start
A Family Than Finish One

Let's look at how important having her parents at home was to my wife, Jeannine. Even though both her parents worked very hard concentrating on making the business successful, the fact that Jeannine and her sisters were only seconds from their parents' side and influence made a great deal of difference in their outlook on life.

It has been our personal mission for the past 13 years to help parents get back home to their families. If you think about it, at the beginning of this century, many families made their livings from their homes — together on the farm. Today, people *want* to go back home and make a living as a family. Even though Jeannine and I didn't have children, we have a real concern and love for kids. Imagine how many children's lives could be turned around for the better if Mom, Dad or both parents made a *sizable, stable income* from home. The home-based business allows the family more time together and personal control over how to use that time. What families do you know who would benefit from that?

Network marketing and, specifically, Nutrition For Life, have given the luxuries of financial freedom and time freedom to hundreds of parents who are stay-at-home moms and dads. People who have always dreamed of having a successful career work from home but never had the right business vehicle to make it happen — that is, until they started their Nutrition For Life business.

Success Secret ...

"The family you come from
   isn't as important as
   the family you create."

PART 4

Don't Wait For Your Ship To Come In ... Swim Out To It!

Dale Brunner,
4-Star Platinum Executive, Wisconsin
Dayle Maloney's "Running Buddy" since 1984
Making The Most Of The Best
And The Least Of The Worst

Dayle Maloney and I were both in a previous network marketing company that went out of business. I was also a realtor at the time. Interest rates soared to over 20% and the market froze. Realtors starved.

My wife, Vickie, and I have 5 children: twins Chanal & Melissa, 24; Nathan, 18; twins Danielle and Nickie, 16.

Back then, my family was *pressed* for money. We put monetary pleasures on the backburner for a while and focused on our long-term financial goals. It got so bad — as much as I don't want to admit it — my family was living on food stamps trying to make ends meet.

After our first network marketing company went out of business, we heard about a small company called Consumer Express in Lake Charles, Louisiana. Following the bad experience with the first company, we had to see this

Consumer Express with our own eyes before we could
recommend it. We traveled to the small corporate
headquarters in Lake Charles to meet the founders, David
Bertrand and Jana Mitcham. We liked what we saw.

Because I had a family to feed — a wife and 5
children — I couldn't fool around. I looked David Bertrand
straight in the eyes and made him promise me two things:
"Promise me you are going to stay in business, and promise
me you will send out bonus checks on time, every month —
forever."

He looked back straight into my eyes and said, "Dale,
I promise you both."

Lake Charles was the same size as the town Dayle and
I lived in, Eau Claire, Wisconsin. I knew because of the size
of the town, some residents would know who David and Jana
were. I walked the town randomly talking to local business
owners. Everyone I asked knew of David, Jana and their
families and spoke highly of them. My own feelings were
confirmed. Dayle Maloney signed up that day and he was my
sponsor.

The network marketing industry has made substantial
advancements in the last decade. When Dayle and I joined, we
had no system to guide us. We paved the way for those who
followed.

While most people were quitting, Dayle and I were
there for each other. *Together we pushed forward.* That was a
big part of our success.

Speaking of Dayle Maloney, here's a guy that was
dealt a lousy hand of cards early on. It could have set the tone

for the rest of his life. As psychologists and teachers will tell you, in most cases, by the time you get to school you've got your outlook on life set by your upbringing and your environment.

Early on, Dayle chose to react positively to every negative situation. It was a *decision* he made. I don't know if it was inherent, but I truly believe that it stems from his <u>ability to dream</u> and the attitude **"I'm going to be somebody. I'm going to prove it. Nobody is going to treat me like that. I'm going to go out and do it."** And he does! Dayle *chooses* to go out and do good, positive, life-changing work. He could have said the same words — "I'm going to be somebody. I'm going to prove it. Nobody is going to treat me like that. I'm going to go out and do it" — but have chosen to *focus* on the *negative* and go out and do destructive work.

It's all a matter of *personal choice.* Notice people use the same words to be constructive or destructive. Both kinds of work are just that ... *work.* Neither one is easier or more difficult than the other. Just work. <u>Just a</u> <u>decision</u>. Just a *point of view*. <u>Both</u> kinds of work could have people telling you <u>to do it</u> and <u>not to do it</u>. Both types of dreams — the positive and the destructive — will have people who want to steal your dream.

It is truly *your choice* which type of work you want to dedicate your life to. <u>You</u> have the **power** and **freedom** of <u>personal</u> <u>choice</u> *regardless* of your situation.

What you *get* out of your chosen work is what you *expect.* Vickie, the kids and I live in a beautiful, spacious debt-free home. As parents, we have always set high expectations for our family. We've never been disappointed! Vickie and I have that same belief in business, and we get great things!

There isn't anybody else in this world that can find more positive in a negative situation than Dayle Maloney. I think it comes from the adversities he faced with an alcoholic father and the traumas that resulted from his father's choices. Dayle rarely talks in detail about it. Then having polio and being told he would never walk again. He just <u>decided</u> to make *every* <u>adversity</u> <u>a</u> <u>positive</u>. Each person has the same personal power, the ability. If you want to enjoy *the most* comfortable life, that is what you do.

Out of respect for Dayle's privacy I will not elaborate on his childhood — all I'll tell you is that most people would never have made it. He won't talk about the details — it's a private thing — but Dayle is proof that people can come out of the *worst* of situations in a positive way with the kind of good heart he has.

By certain standards there is every indication that Dayle Maloney should have been *a loser, a failure, a trouble maker* — a kid that got in trouble with the law. Instead, he made the <u>choice</u> <u>in</u> <u>his</u> <u>mind</u> to go *just the opposite*. That's all it was, *a choice* in his own mind — his own personal power. You have that choice and can exercise it. It is *never* too late.

Dayle talks about having an "I will succeed in spite of list." He has a long list of people who *never* believed he would amount to anything. Dayle always told me he would prove to his dad that he was, "Going to be somebody because of it all — in spite of it all."

Whatever Dayle had to do, he was going to do it. When Dayle Maloney makes up his mind to do something — *don't* bet against him.

Dayle became a survivor — a total compassionate,

passionate human being. Because of the pain Dayle has experienced in his past, he goes out of his way to diminish or reduce pain and suffering for other people. That is why he is so compassionate to children.

Dayle is living proof that great results come from having a dream and searching for a way to accomplish your dream — regardless of your current situation. Your dream is what will keep you alive and bring you through it all.

Vickie and Dale Brunner

Success Secret ...

> "Remember, success is a good teacher;
> challenge is a better teacher.
> Success pampers the mind;
> challenge trains and strengthens it."

PART 5

Dayle, Why Did You Pick Network Marketing?

Not so much now that I have the kind of success I do, but for years when I was just getting started, people asked, "Why did you pick network marketing?"

You see, at that point in my life I was over *$250,000 in debt*. I was driving down the road one day and I heard this patriotic music and the announcement over the radio waves: "Come and hear Zig Ziglar, Dr. Norman Vincent Peale, Paul Harvey, Earl Nightingale...!" The list went on and on. *I was so excited!*

Money was tight but I went out and bought two $15.00 tickets. The event was held at the Met Sports Center in Bloomington, Minnesota. Jeannine and I went together. It was a total sellout — 15,000 people! I did a quick calculation in my mind taking 15,000 people times $15 each and realized that's $225,000! I turned to Jeannine and proclaimed, "I know how we can get out of debt in *one* day! *We'll* do the *same thing* over in St. Paul, right across the river!" And we did.

My event was called the *Dare To Succeed Rally*. I had a theater-in-the round — 17,711 seats. I had a big line up of speakers for the event: Dr. Wayne Dyer, Dr. Norman Vincent Peale, Art Linkletter, Bob Richards, Janet Guthrie, and Joe Girard — the world's greatest salesman.

I was so excited to have finally figured out how Jeannine and I were going to prosper and how I could keep the promise I made to Jeannine's mother that was burning in the back of my mind. Remember the promise I made the day of our wedding? I agreed that I would be a good provider.

My heart could hardly take the wait as I imagined in my hands more cash than I had ever seen at one time. The day of the event finally arrived.

We took a tally and had sold only 7,500 tickets. We had over 10,000 empty seats. My financial victory was a financial disaster. You see, that day I lost another $91,000. Jeannine and I were now over $350,000 in debt.

The morning after the rally I realized the people who made all the money were *the speakers*. <u>They got all the money</u>. I told my wife, "As of today, I have become a public speaker."

But I didn't have any bookings. So I called a consultant in California, Howard Shenson. I said, " Howard, I want to do some public seminars." This guy convinced me my seminar should be called *Secrets Of How To Be A Public Speaker*. It sounded a little strange, since I hadn't figured out any of those secrets myself!

But Howard assured me it would sell like hot cakes.

He told me I should do my first show in Omaha, Nebraska. Howard said, "Charge them $95, give them a workbook, take two breaks, offer them free beverages, soft drinks, tea, donuts and things."

"How big of a crowd will it be, Howard?" I asked.

"Run the ad I told you and you'll have about 200 people," he replied.

To seat 200 people conference style requires a ballroom. So I was in Omaha at the Airport Ramada Inn. I had the ads in the paper and I had two assistants to help me handle 200 people.

The day of the event came. **TWO** people showed up. One guy thought it was too hot in the room. The other guy thought it was too cold. They fought over the thermostat. One guy had a Diners Club Card. I didn't even know what it was and I didn't take those — but I took it that night. The other guy gave me a bad check.

Now think of this. The biggest fear someone has — bigger than flying or dying — is what? National studies show it is *public speaking* but at the time *I didn't know that*. So I tried a second one. I ventured to St. Louis, Missouri, to the Marriott at the Airport. First Class all the way!

Only two showed up.

I was still dumb enough to try it again. The third one I held in Cleveland, Ohio, at the Sheraton at the John Hopkins Airport. I had one person show up that night. I needed his $95 *so bad* that I took him to a little booth in the coffee shop, and I trained him how to be a public speaker. I wasn't one myself, yet.

I changed the seminar to *The Secrets of Selling* and went back on the road. I started to draw people. Not huge crowds — usually between 20 and 50 people. I started to make enough money to live seminar-to-seminar but not enough to start paying off much of the $350,000 debt. I gave these seminars all over the country. My wife, Jeannine, often traveled with me.

While we were on the road together, our home in White Bear Lake was burglarized. They cleaned us out — took everything we owned. We were mortified when we arrived home and walked into the house.

Jeannine didn't feel safe there anymore so we moved to a 3rd floor apartment in St. Paul, Minnesota. We hopped back on the road to do more seminars. When we returned home, we found what very little we had accumulated since the last burglary — had been stolen. We had nothing *again*.

I'd like to say things got better, but *they didn't*. Shortly afterwards, we were evicted because at age 47, I couldn't afford to pay $425 a month rent for my wife and me. We were homeless. I asked Jeannine to call her mother and ask if we could move in with her that night.

Because we were living seminar-to-seminar, we had to get back out on the road. Jeannine decided to stay home. So I went out alone most of the time.

Two weeks after my wife and I got evicted, the engine in my old junker blew up. (That car was so bad that every time I filled up the gas tank, I increased its value.) I couldn't afford to have the engine fixed. I called my mother-in-law and asked if I could use her car. By this time I was in debt over my head. The *only* thing I owned at that time was <u>a dream</u> to pay off every creditor before I died. I *somehow* wanted to get out from under the bondage of debt. I knew I could never do that by getting a job. I'd have to work 3 or 4 jobs until I was 136 years old, and I didn't think I'd live that long. I had to get back out on the road hoping *somehow* to make enough money.

Jeannine was driving me to the airport to fly to a *Secrets of Selling Seminar* I was doing in San Diego, California. Right down on Snelling Avenue in St. Paul here came a car out of a side street and into the driver's side of our car. Oh, man!

Jeannine was scared, but by some miracle she wasn't hurt. After we were done with the police, I said, "Drive me to the airport. I've got to get going."

I barely made the flight to San Diego. In those days, we were always one seminar away from starving. Really, it was that bad. In those days there wasn't really an overnight package delivery service. There was something called Express Mail. One night I did a seminar in Riverside, California. After the seminar ended at 10 p.m., I gathered my money together and I drove as fast as I could all the way into Los Angeles to the LAX Airport. I paid to get that money counter-to-counter on Western Airlines on the 1 a.m. red eye. I had to get it back to St. Paul at 6:30 a.m. so Jeannine could pick up the money at the airport. We *couldn't even wait* one extra day for a courier service. That's how bad it was. It was just terribly hard. That's why I did so many seminars in the Los Angeles and San Francisco areas — so I could get the money sent back on the red-eye flights.

At the time, we didn't realize how bad it really was. We were just busy doing it. Sometimes I'd be out on the road myself for three or four weeks straight presenting 11 seminars a week — two each day, Monday through Friday, and one on Saturday. I'm sure that people who attended my seminars could tell by my clothes that I wasn't really successful. I'd wear those clothes to the threads. I'd have no choice. Buying a new suit was a big thing.

Why didn't I just quit? My polio taught me that when you feel like giving up, that's when you're over half way to success.

Success Secret ...

> "The *difference* between a successful person and others is *not* a lack of strength, *not* a lack of knowledge, but *rather* a lack of will."

PART 6

Never Deprive Someone Of Hope, It May Be All They Have

In February, 1983, as people were leaving after one of the seminars I presented in Portland, Oregon, I saw a woman handing my attendees an audio tape. After all the people were gone I approached her to find out what was going on. She told me she was just handing out a free audio tape. She told me it was network marketing and asked me if I wanted one. "No," I laughed, "I'm not at all interested in that."

"Well, I see in the newspaper that you're in Seattle next week. I'm from Seattle. Can I come to your next seminars and hand out tapes at the end?" she asked.

"Yes, but keep it low keyed and just don't be a pest to my people," I said. I just couldn't say no to her because I knew what it was like to try to get a business going.

I was setting up the second of two seminars in Seattle when a gentleman approached me. I recognized him from the seminar the day before. I was excited. Maybe he had come back to purchase the audio tape program I was offering. "Yes, sir. How can I help you?" I asked.

"Is the woman here who handed out the free tape last night?" He asked excitedly.

"No sir, those weren't my tapes but the woman said she would be back tonight. You're welcome to come back," I replied. This puzzled me.

That evening the "tape lady" returned and handed out free tapes again. I saw the man come back to see her. After the seminar, I asked her exactly what she was doing. She explained it was network marketing and asked me if I wanted a tape. I took one and packed up for the night. The only problem was I had a rental car that didn't have a tape player.

I had a good friend in Spokane, Pat Johnson. I called and asked her to listen to a tape I was going to send her explaining I had no clue what it was about. Pat must have listened because she immediately called Jeannine back in Wisconsin and left a message that it was urgent I call her.

I returned Pat's call and she said to me, "I want to sign up."

I gasped, "What?"

She repeated, "I want to sign up."

I couldn't believe my ears. So I called the "tape lady" and inquired, "What do I do?" She sent me applications and more tapes. So I got Pat signed up. *That meant I had to sign up*. It was March 1, 1983 and I had opened my eyes to network marketing.

I still didn't know what was on the tape. I handed the tape to another fella and the same thing happened. He called Jeannine at home and left a message: "Tell Dayle I want in."

I called my sponsor: "What do I do to get started in the business?"

She said, "Sponsor as many people as you can as fast as you can in the next 31 days." Friend, <u>every</u> <u>morning</u> <u>is</u> <u>the</u> <u>start</u> <u>of</u> <u>your</u> <u>next</u> <u>31</u> <u>days</u>.

Success Secret ...

"Don't you *ever, ever, ever* quit sponsoring new people yourself."

PART 7

The Best Way To Predict The Future Is To Create It

My sponsor told me once I got back to Wisconsin to have a home meeting and hand the tapes out there.

I couldn't wait to get home to tell my wife and mother-in-law — (I had to answer to the *two* of them now). I announced, "I know how we're going to get out of debt!"

My wife scowled, "How?"

She was kind of negative, and I couldn't blame her. I said, "We're going to do it in network marketing. They also call it MLM."

Her exact words were, "I married you for better or for worse but not for one of *those* things." She stayed with me all those years but at that moment, I couldn't have blamed her if she had left. I had become the master of economic disaster and my latest proposed venture was taking her well out of her comfort zone.

I said, "What do you mean?"

She said, "Those things kind of *embarrass* me."

I said, "Being broke embarrasses me a whole lot more!"

I had no choice; I had to go for it. When I decided I would move forward, I made a promise with myself that I would live by 6 words: <u>DON'T</u> <u>EVER</u> <u>LEARN</u> <u>HOW</u> <u>TO</u> <u>QUIT</u>.

Success Secret ...

> "Winners never quit.
> Quitters never win."

Obstacles Are Those Frightful Things You See When You Stop Focusing On Your Goals

I got all set to go to work that first night. I told my wife, as I was sitting at my mother-in-law's kitchen table, "My sponsor told me to make up my prospect list."

She said, "Wait ahhh *minute! Before* you make up your list, I'm going to make up my list of the people you're *not* allowed to talk to."

It was the biggest "unprospect" list I've ever seen: no relatives, no friends, no one we went to school with, nobody I worked with, and nobody that lived within 100 miles of Eau Claire, Wisconsin. I didn't care, I was going for it!

I invited 30 people to a home meeting at my mother-in-law's house. I didn't sleep for two nights worrying how I was ever going to get 30 chairs in the lower level family room. I shouldn't have worried about it because only *two* showed up. I just got started with the meeting and the one man said, " Is the restroom handy?"

"Yes, Sir, it's at the top of the steps," I directed. He never returned. The second man couldn't see the opportunity. I didn't sponsor anyone that night.

I tried one more home meeting and invited 20 people. None of them showed but one of the 20 sent his friend, the dishwasher at Kentucky Fried Chicken. About 21 years old, he came right from work wearing a paper hat with Colonel Sander's picture on it which said, "Colonel Sander's Kentucky Fried." Across his T-shirt it read, "We make chicken better." He still wore the apron from work.

He probably hadn't taken a bath for a while. Within a matter of 5 minutes the entire house smelled of pure Kentucky Fried. You know, that's a good smell. He smelled so good and it made me so hungry, I wanted to gnaw on him.

He left because he couldn't see the opportunity. Driving away he made so much noise because his car had no muffler. My wife unlocked the bedroom door and came out sniffin'. She said, "Oh, great! You went out and picked up some Kentucky Fried."

I said, "No that's the man that just left." In those day's Kentucky Fried's slogan said their chicken was, "Finger Lickin' Good". We were so broke, we would have had to lick someone else's fingers.

I've had hundreds of reasons to quit. Let's face it … we all have. *Don't ever* learn how to quit. I had *many* tough times. I'd have to say to myself, "I'd rather *die trying* than be *called a quitter*."

Friend, if you have sponsored one person into this business, you have given up the right to quit. Somebody thought enough of you to say, "Hey, I want you to bring me into the business." If you've got one person sponsored, you no longer have the right to quit. In this industry this is really not an opportunity; it is a responsibility.

I hear people all the time. Oh, they've got "tough-times." I was guilty of it, too. They say, "We keep telling God about all our problems." TRY THIS INSTEAD! Some day sit down and tell *your problems* how big your God is! It makes a BIG difference in business and in life.

Be sure you see people where they *want to go* — not where they have *been*. I never ask anybody for a resume. I ask them, "Have you got a dream?" You look at where they *could be*. Not where they've *been*. The number one success ingredient in Nutrition For Life is you have to have a dream.

You're going to have to get out there and you'll have to make a promise to yourself that, "I'll be easy to start and hard to stop." **Don't give your business what you've got, give it what it takes**. If Dale Brunner and I gave this business *what we had*, we wouldn't be here today. We gave it *whatever it took*. I've got a saying I've followed for years ... "Hard work is the yeast that raises the $$$dough$$$."

Now people are going to ridicule you and say, "Oh, you're so dumb. You're stupid for working that business."

They still tell *me* I'm stupid to work this business. I guess that makes me $7,000,000.00 and counting stupid, huh? When somebody tells you you're stupid, you've got two choices. You can go to work and prove them wrong ... or you can agree with them and quit. When they say you're stupid, **you go to work and prove them wrong!** That's where it's at.

It wasn't easy for me. The truth is it probably won't be easy for you, either. The road to success is always under construction. But *you have the right* in the Free World to *fight for your freedom!* The only thing *easy* in life is *failure*. But you'll pay for failure the rest of your life.

My mother-in-law's house, where Jeannine and I moved in after I couldn't pay $425 a month to keep our apartment, is where my network marketing career was launched.

Success Secret ...

"Failure is not important unless it's the last time you're going to try."

PART 9

The Eternal Optimist

David Bertrand, President And CEO,
Nutrition For Life International
Attitude And Belief Will Determine The Outcome

When Nutrition For Life's Executive Vice-President Jana Mitcham and I first started out in 1984 in Lake Charles, Louisiana, we were undercapitalized and flying by the seat of our pants. We were successful, seasoned network marketers who did not realize how much money was required to start a company. Instead of money, we operated on the huge dream of what this company could be.

In the beginning, we had a couple of very exciting years where we grew quickly and because of that growth in the mid-1980's we ran out of capital. We couldn't afford to print good 4-color literature, our success kits needed improvement and we couldn't offer the support our distributors in the field desired. Our company, like many companies in our industry, fell into some hard times.

Most companies, that went through what we did, are out of business today. When a company hits its peak and lacks growth capital, most owners bail out scrambling for other things to do. They are not totally committed to their dream or their people. It never entered our minds that we should have closed the company when things weren't going as well as they are today. Our attitude was to fix whatever needed fixing and make it work.

We were 100% totally committed to succeeding regardless of the price. We knew what we wanted to accomplish. No matter what happened we were committed to staying in business. Even today, Jana and I believe when we make a commitment we must do everything we can to make sure that commitment is fulfilled.

I believe the single most valuable commodity we have in this business is trust. There is only one way to have trust ... by earning it. Network marketing distributors are volunteers, not employees — they don't have to join. They follow us because they believe in us. We are in the trust business.

Jana and I have worked very, very hard from day one to be individuals of honesty and integrity by only making promises which we can deliver upon. People must be able to look the officers of a network marketing company straight in the eye and know they can trust those people.

We want the people out in the field to see that we are not wasting their money. We have a nice office but it is not extravagant. We always travel commercially. We have never had a private plane to bring us here or there. We would rather put the company money into building the company to make sure the business is solid and people receive their bonus checks.

Nutrition For Life has a stable business structure, an excited field force and good product offerings. We are poised to enter the momentum stage. Whether we grow to be the largest network marketing company is not a concern, but we will be a major company with a great reputation.

We were most recently voted as one of the permanent members of the Direct Selling Association (DSA), an organization of about 60 members of which about 70% are network marketing companies. To be selected, a company must endure intense scrutiny from the DSA board. What makes their scrutiny tough is that they know network marketing very well and know what to look for. It speaks well to have been chosen to be a member of the DSA.

We are also proud of Nutrition For Life's pattern of strong growth. In 1993, Nutrition For Life sales were $12 million and in 1994, we grew to $17 ½ million. In 1995, we were well on our way to a $25 million year when mid-way through 1995, Kevin Trudeau joined our organization and we jumped to sales of $32 million.

Kevin came in with a lot of excitement and enlightened us. He is a big dreamer and caused Jana, Dayle and me to expand our dreams and thoughts of what we were capable of doing. From $32 million in gross sales we grew to $97 million the following year. Kevin caused excitement and many more great people to join Nutrition For Life.

The growth of a network marketing company is never on the shoulders of any one person. Dayle, Jana, Kevin, our current distributor base and I acted as catalysts to sponsor additional good people.

The number of people joining our industry is growing daily and it has a great future. Internationally, over $70 billion in goods and services are sold through network marketing each year. On a worldwide basis, over 21 million people are distributors including over 8 million in the United States. In my opinion, network marketing is the final frontier for financial freedom in this country.

Where is Nutrition For Life positioned in the industry? We are prepared to handle incredible growth. When is it going to hit? It could be three months, could be the first of next year ... who knows? What we want is long-term, steady, sustainable growth. We'd love to see a 30% to 50% growth factor per year.

Dayle Maloney has played a key role in the growth of this company. We often talk about Nutrition For Life being built on core values: freedom, equality, individual worth, love. Dayle Maloney epitomizes all of those values. He is Mr. Freedom, Mr. Equality.

If you want to work the business, Dayle will help you. He is equality. He sees deep into people and discovers levels of worthiness that nobody else sees. Dayle Maloney loves people and people just love him. He is such an integral part of what we do, and I have an incredible respect for him.

As a result of the love he has for people, Dayle's schedule is hectic. Often times, over the years, we have said, "Hey Dayle what if you slow down a little bit?"

"Okay, no problem," he'll agree.

Then we'll be holding a Saturday night meeting and Dayle will say, "Hey, David, before the Saturday night meeting, how about swinging over to visit this Friday night group over here? It sure would help them, and it's on the way, so we might as well do it."

I agree and before we leave for the Friday night meeting, Dayle has me convinced to stop by a Thursday night meeting. Before I know it, we are touring the country with a full week of meetings.

I used to remind him, "Dayle, you are not as young as you were. You must slow down a little bit and start pacing yourself." I don't tell him that anymore. I suddenly realized Nutrition For Life is his life. He loves being on the road, being with the people.

Once Dayle and Jeannine decided to take a vacation to Nassau for a week. Dayle was on the beautiful beach ... and there was *no phone*. He called me and said, "David, this is the worst experience I have ever had in my life. I will never come back here. I am so miserable without a phone."

Dayle will never slow down and if he ever did, it would be bad for him. This business is his hobby, his life, his passion — he loves it and wouldn't want to do anything else.

When Dayle first joined Nutrition For Life, his generosity did not come from having money. Dayle gave to others when he didn't have anything to give. He lived by the universal principle, "The more you give, the more you receive."

Dayle is a very spiritual person. He believes God will take care of him: "If I help this person, look what they can become." Dayle was and still is generous because of the love he has for people and his desire to help people be all they can be.

I've witnessed Dayle sharing his time, energy and love, even when he didn't have it to give. He gives because he loves to give. His generosity towards people has increased as his money has increased. Dayle is wealthy because he loves people.

Dayle will never, ever again be broke. He has thousands of friends who love him, which is a wealth that cannot be described in dollars.

He is viewed and will be remembered as a man who did great things for other people. There is no pedestal high enough, angelic enough, or glamorous enough that would do justice to Dayle Maloney. I think the pedestal Dayle Maloney sits upon is in the hearts of thousands of people whose lives he has touched. I believe that is exactly where he wants to be.

Many people have asked, "Dayle, when are you going to retire?"

Dayle responds, "I'll tell you when I am going to retire, when they throw the dirt over my coffin. That is when I will retire."

I never can see a time when Dayle would walk away from this business. Maybe someday he will appear at fewer meetings, but as long as he has a pulse, he'll always be involved.

Dayle has created such a lasting impression in people that years after he is gone, he will have an influence. Eventually, we all go to a better place. As we travel through this life, the best we can hope for is to leave a positive impression in the hearts of people, so after we are gone, they can remember us fondly and our influence will live on. I know more than 100,000 people who will remember Dayle Maloney with love and respect.

I think Dayle has a tremendous number of meetings, presentations, speeches and business building activities left in him. But when his time does come, I can just envision that first shovel of dirt going over the coffin and a knock coming from inside saying, "Wait a minute! I have a call I want to make to Bertrand."

Nutrition For Life Co-Founders
Executive Vice-President Jana Mitcham and
President and CEO David Bertrand

Success Secret...

"Whether you think you can or you think you can't, you are right."

PART 10

Do It Now!

Rosemary Hunt,
1-Star Platinum Executive, Canada
If You Can Dream It, You Can Do It

I joined Nutrition For Life in September, 1992. Prior to that, it was discovered that at age 19, my son, Kal, had an inoperable brain tumor. I joined NFL in order to purchase the products at wholesale which we needed to restore his health. I believe we don't have to die from cancer if it is caught in the early stages. I believe the Nutrition For Life products and especially the shark cartilage, along with prayer and will-power built my son's immune system up so strong that he was able to survive. It was a miracle.

While I was struggling with my son's cancer, I was called into the personnel office and *told I no longer had a job.* I worked for the Canadian government for 30 years and was not even making $2,000 a month. I was at the point where I *knew* I had to do *something different.* The job I loved for so many years had gone sour when new management took over.

They offered me a buy-out. It was a real turmoil for me because I was used to working at a job for 30 years. My stomach turned on March 31, 1994 when I walked out the door for the final time after all those years.

From September, 1992 to March, 1994, I had worked my Nutrition For Life business very part-time.

On April 1st, the first day after my buy-out, I placed all my career focus on my Nutrition for Life business. I knew I had to do it. I had no choice but to succeed. I was a single parent and we lived off my income. The buy-out had left me with 7 months salary to live on to build my NFL business. Five months later, in August, 1994, I had earned a new car from Nutrition For Life.

It took me sponsoring people and helping those people succeed to make the business work. You can't just focus on yourself and say, "Oh, I'm going to get this car." Instead you need to say, "I'm going to help as many people as possible and the car will come."

Success comes from doing home meetings, working one-on-one with people, showing them how to build their belief level while you're building your own. To succeed you must work with your people to show them exactly how to use the system of success Nutrition For Life offers to build their business. I spend a good deal of time helping others find confidence within themselves which helps me find the same within myself. My own personal growth catapults as I teach others.

The personal growth a person will experience with Nutrition for Life is phenomenal. You will realize you have so much potential inside! You'll discover you have the personal power to conquer anything! Personal growth will come before financial growth. You'll get wealthy in the mind before you'll get wealthy in the wallet.

In two years in my Nutrition For Life business I was making *far more* each month than my monthly salary after *working for 30 years*. In my J-O-B, I needed to go to work *every day* to earn my salary. In contrast with my Nutrition For Life business, for two years I needed to focus on my business, and now I receive my checks even if I take a month off.

Do you want 30 years tied to a job or do you want two to five years focusing on an investment that will pay you forever, regardless if you are working it or not? It's your choice. Why not choose long-term residual income and get paid every month for the rest of your life.

I took my son to Mexico for cancer treatments for seven months. *Seven months*, I was gone concentrating on keeping my son alive. For *seven months* I did *not* work my Nutrition For Life business. What do you think happened to my check? **_It went up!_** *It's true*.

Try that in a job or with most any other business. After 7 months of being gone, what would you expect to return to? Ruins.

Each month for *all* those 7 months, my check came to my mailbox. It was deposited and each month — while I was in Mexico with my son fighting for his life — my check grew bigger and bigger.

Worldwide it's no secret the Canadian HealthCare system leaves something to be desired. To treat my son cost over $50,000. Do you know what insurance covered that? My monthly Nutrition for Life check. It's the best insurance I could have.

In Canada, like other countries, we make sure our Nutrition For Life business owners receive training on the different network marketing compensation plans available to them. This helps them realize what they have with Nutrition For Life. We take the basic marketing plans like breakaways, binaries, and uni-levels and then compare them with my 4 x 7 Nutrition For Life business on a visual chart. There isn't even a close comparison.

We illustrate what would have happened to my income if I had been in any other type of program. The result? Slim chance that I would have gotten checks when I was in Mexico for 7 months to save my son. That's important to know. You want to build your network marketing business *once* and be able to walk away. If you have a crisis in your life you want the freedom to deal with it knowing your check - *your income* - will be there. No other company will offer you that. Trust me, I know that.

Today I have more than 500 people in my downline and 17 are driving cars for which Nutrition For Life is making the monthly car payments.

**Rosemary Hunt (center)
with son, Kal and daughter, Rhonda**

Success Secret ...

"If you are just too busy to help
the people around you succeed,
you are just too busy."

PART 11

Never Ask, "*Can* I Do This?" Rather Ask, "*How* Can I Do This?"

Peter Angell, 4-Star Platinum Executive, Florida
A Mentor Helps Others Find
What Is Already In Their Hearts

When I became involved with Nutrition For Life in June of 1995, I was excited to meet Dayle Maloney because I had heard so much wonderful information about him. I also knew he was making over $100,000 a month in the *exact business* I just started!

When I first was introduced to him I immediately felt he was one of the nicest, most compassionate and caring people I had ever met. Very low keyed, non-pretentious — just salt-of-the-earth — would do anything for you kind-of-guy. I was honored to be able to mentor with him and listen to him.

Dayle's messages ring loud and clear throughout the network marketing community: Work with the people you have. Be persistent and committed. Don't ever, ever quit. Keep going.

How did I build my business? I selected to work with people who I wanted on my "board of directors" — people whose experience and opinion I respected enough to base the success of my business on.

Who would those people be? I targeted people who were go-getters. People who would go the extra mile. It could have been a teacher, a minister, just someone who had that "go-getting" type of attitude.

You might be a little uncomfortable at first picking up the phone to talk to them about the business. When I train people in my organization how to do this, I tell them, I will be there with you — either by phone or in person — sitting next to you, to assist you with the first 10 to 15 people who are on your board of directors list. I tell them, "You own your own business, but you're not alone in it."

How do you open a conversation with a person who you have never talked to about business before? And what if you're not even known as a business person, then what? One of the really nice things about Nutrition For Life is the training program. Tapes that tell you exactly what to say.

Because of the integrity of President David Bertrand, Executive Vice-President Jana Mitcham, and Dayle Maloney, I have done a little closer examination of who I am as a person and how I want others to view me. Working with these people, I have to look in the mirror pretty closely and make sure who I see staring back is somebody I want to have as my best friend. If that's not the case then ask them for help. They'll give you the tools to change that situation. They will give you what you need to get what you want.

Dayle's been in the network marketing industry a decade. I just hope when I've been in the business for the same number of years as Dayle, I will have the fine quality reputation. As you know, the network marketing industry does not always have people of integrity in it. When you have someone who's been in the business for a good number of years and has continued to exemplify honesty, compassion and commitment — it speaks well for the entire industry. Those who have been in the industry for a long time know that. Dayle Maloney is a wonderful figurehead for the network marketing industry.

What kind of a mentor is Dayle? I was visiting him in Wisconsin along with two others, Wydell and Loretta Madison both from California. Wydell and I were there to observe Dayle holding an opportunity meeting. Before we knew it, Wydell and I were doing the meeting! I don't know how that happened, but before we knew it, we were in front of the people.

Peter Angell, a single mother, now makes a
sizable monthly income and her daughter has been
able to graduate from college debt-free!

Success Secret ...

"Your dreams should be grand enough
to get the best of you."

PART 12

Home Is Where
The Heart Is

Dallas & Kathy Swanstrom, Wisconsin
When You Go To Work You Shouldn't
Have To Leave Your Family At Home

My wife, Kathy, met Dayle in 1961 when he started dating her sister, Jeannine. I started dating Kathy in 1965 and met Dayle then. In 1961 when Kathy was in 7th grade, she started assembling mailings for Dayle. As we sit here today, over 35 years later, we are right now putting together a mailing for him.

Our whole family works at Dayle's Nutrition For Life distribution center. Dayle sees the big picture and gathers others around him to work the details. When he gets going on something, Dayle wants things to move quickly. He is very enthusiastic, and it rubs off on the people.

Kathy and I joined Nutrition For Life in 1992. I've had the blessing of helping Dayle with many of the seminars he offers. I've been many miles with Nutrition For Life President David Bertrand and Executive Vice-President Jana Mitcham. I've discovered what great people they are, honest and upright. I have never heard them say a bad word about any distributor.

Dayle has been so generous to our family. Kathy and I have a son, Dana, and two daughters, Tara and Tessa. Tara is married to our son-in-law, Tracy Ternberg. In the last 15 years for every Christmas except one or two, Dayle and Jeannine have taken our family someplace for the holidays. We've been to Hawaii four or five times, to Florida, the Bahamas, California, etc. Dayle and Jeannine have no children. They treat our kids like they would their own — and mom and dad get to go along!

Dayle is very independent and even though his eyesight isn't the best, he loves to drive. Dayle had a scare when he renewed his drivers license and had to take the vision test. The examiner asked Dayle to look into the machine and, "Tell me what you see."

Dayle worried out loud, "I can't see a thing."

The examiner adjusted the machine and again Dayle said, "I still can't see a thing."

This went on for awhile until the examiner finally came around and discovered the light bulb was burned out in the machine. Much to Dayle's relief, he passed the test.

It is a wonderful experience to know Dayle. He has been a blessing to our family.

My wife, Kathy, was at the Reno Clinic for 2 weeks. Dayle was also there. When Dayle checked out of the Reno Clinic, he paid Kathy's bill.

Our son, daughters and son-in-law all drive new cars free because of Dayle and Nutrition For Life. In 1965, I never guessed the positive impact Nutrition For Life would have on our family. Today, I know it is possible to bring your business home to where the heart is.

Dallas and Kathy Swanstrom's Family

Back Row: son, Dana; daughter, Tessa; son-in-law, Tracy Ternberg; foreign exchange student, Peter

Middle Row: Dallas; Kathy; daughter, Tara Ternberg; Jeannine

Seated: Dayle

PART 13

The Church

Pastor Dale Johnson,
Friendship Church, Mondovi, Wisconsin
It Is Well To Give When Asked,
But It Is Exceptional To Give Unasked

I have been Dayle's pastor at Friendship Baptist Church in Mondovi, Wisconsin since August, 1992.

Dayle is a "mover and a shaker" who makes things happen. We held church in a rented facility, a store front that had been a lumber yard. Dayle and Jeannine made a significant donation which helped us build our new church. Before Jeannine's mother, Maxine, passed on, she prayed someday our church would occupy the lot behind her house. In 1994, Jeannine used her inheritance from her mother to help purchase a lot for the church.

In July, 1995, Jeannine and Dayle donated to our church 10,000 shares of Nutrition For Life stock. At the time, it was selling at less than $6 a share. Dayle believed the stock would increase in value so we began to develop building plans, and contractors were bidding the job. By November 1995, the stock had increased to $37.50 a share and later $41.25. We sold the stock at both points and raised a total of more than $400,000. Dayle and Jeannine's generosity exceeded my expectations. They are proof of how God's tremendous miracles are displayed through humans.

Sometimes, people with money try to throw their weight around by trying to dictate the type of building or the building location. It is to Dayle and Jeannine's credit that they only made one simple request: could Jeannine's mother, who had been a real prayer warrior in this church, have one room named in her honor?

Today, the "Maxine Miller Fireside Room" is a small fellowship room where people can meet. Dayle and Jeannine's only request was to honor Jeannine's mother. We were more than delighted to do so. There is a simple plaque dedicating the room to Maxine that does not even have Dayle and Jeannine Maloney's name on it.

Through all this, most of our congregation members are not aware Dayle is a public speaker. They have no idea how well-known, loved and appreciated Dayle is outside of our circle.

As you develop a relationship with Dayle, his consistency and depth show through. You respect him more-and-more, rather than less-and-less. I have seen a side of Dayle where he faces criticism, pressure in his business, or experiences a real blow where something hits him hard. He has the ability to recover, stabilize and move on. Not everybody does. There is more to Dayle Maloney than meets the eye. I have a great deal of respect for him, and I appreciate him very much.

**Pastor Dale Johnson and
his lovely wife Amy**

The Friendship Church

Success Secret ...

"You make a living by what you receive;
you make a life but what you give."

PART 14

If You Want A Great Team, Be A Great Teammate

Jim and Jo Leyde,
4-Star Platinum Executives, Oregon
You Are Just One Good Distributor Away
From A Fortune

The *first thing* you need to do when you start your Nutrition For Life business is to take the product catalog, go through your house and take an inventory to see what products you are using now — that you could be buying from *your own store*. We think it amazes anyone who does that.

When Jo and I did this we found 52 products in our house we replenish monthly. Forty-seven of them could have been bought from us — our own store, Nutrition For Life.

The first thing this does is let you understand you are not buying anything new. The products keep people involved in their business. The products fulfill people's needs and expectations.

Your next step is to have a home meeting as fast as you can. We present the home meeting for our new distributors. They need to have one or two home meetings within their first week, if possible.

This will lead to helping your new distributor sponsor at least one person. Work with that new distributor until that distributor can go out and do the same thing. Rather than going out and trying to sign up 5 or 6 people, where you can't work with any of them properly, just sponsor and work with one person at a time. Work with that one person until that one person *can duplicate* what you have done. Then sponsor a second person.

Some people get in this rat race where they think they need to go out and sponsor 50 people immediately. What happens is a few months down the road they look at the printout and wonder why there are only a few people left. It's because the sponsor hasn't done his or her job.

Your job is to sponsor one person and help that person learn to do the same again and again. Dayle Maloney has always said this and it is true: "One good distributor can be worth $5,000 to $25,000 a month to you." *One good distributor.* So it's worth taking the time to work with that one good distributor and build relationships. You can't do this business long-term without building relationships.

It's simplest to start in your own backyard with the people you can get to in 20 minutes, that's your market. Go across the street before you start going down the street. When you start out you can give the best support to local people. You can't help but go nationally and even internationally. It just happens because this person talks to that person. We have downlines in the Philippines and Guam even though we have never been there.

Some people think they are going to get a pot of gold overnight in network marketing. If they don't make their first million in 6 months they want to quit — that's silly.

We never suggest anyone quit their job until they have done this for at least one year and for at least a year their *monthly* income more than equals what their paycheck was each month.

Years ago, before Jo and I started our Nutrition For Life Business, we were really fed up with this industry. Out of 175,000 distributors in our previous company we were number one and the company went bankrupt on us.

I thought, "How could this possibly have happened?" I met with Dayle and found out he had the same type of experience where his first company went bankrupt.

Dayle Maloney said Nutrition For Life was different. In my mind when I considered Nutrition For Life, *the only reason* this company was different was because *Dayle Maloney* said it was different.

All distributors say their company is the best, but I could see in Dayle that he had the ability to stick with it. He was going to be there no matter what and wasn't out to feed me a bunch of baloney about what was going to happen. Dayle just said he would be there for Jo and me, and through all the years, he has kept his word.

Wherever Dayle is, people will follow because of his credibility.

Dayle Maloney is what makes Nutrition For Life different from the other network marketing opportunities.

Dayle did not talk MLM-ese — that slick jargon or lingo that some use in the industry. That talk just takes away from the credibility of the company. Dayle didn't do that. He's what made it different when we were looking at companies.

Being proven leaders, we were well aware of and could have chosen *any* company in the industry. We chose Nutrition For Life because of Dayle Maloney.

I don't think Nutrition For Life would be anything near the company it is today without Dayle Maloney. The network marketing industry usually tends to evaluate the effectiveness of a company by the money people make. I don't think that is always the best measure. I think if you look back and see the lives that were saved — physically, emotionally and financially — because of Nutrition For Life and Dayle Maloney, then you could fairly evaluate the impact.

So many of the network marketing companies are designed for only a few at the top — who came in first — to make the big money. That's not the case here. We have people who came in *years* after we did — who are making good money. That will continue to hold true for people who come in for years to come and use the system to build their business.

If you met Dayle Maloney in a group of a thousand people, you wouldn't know he had a penny. You'd just know he's honorable — somebody you just enjoy talking with — somebody you like being around.

And we have to remember, Dayle Maloney wouldn't be where he is or who he is without someone like his wife, Jeannine, behind him.

Most wives probably wouldn't tolerate what she did

when he first started. He worked twenty-eight hours a day, 8 days a week.

In the early years, unlike now, you didn't make much in this company no matter how hard you worked. It took a long, long time and she stuck with him and gave him support. A lot of spouses wouldn't have done that. And Jeannine is as generous as Dayle is.

Success Secret ...

"What is the secret of network marketing success? Sponsor one person. Help that person learn to do the same, then duplicate the secret over and over."

PART 15

To Get The Best The World Has To Offer, Give The Best

I've always chosen to be a giver. I just do it. I've always been that way. I've been hurt a lot of times — where people take advantage of me — but I just keep on doing it. I believe we're supposed to be givers and not takers. I think if there is one thing the network industry is short on — I'm not talking about Nutrition For Life — I'm talking about the industry in general. It is short on givers and way heavy on takers. Lots of takers in this industry. Take, take, take. That's why these people jump from company-to-company.

The only dark side of network marketing is the thousands of people who sit in their homes on the phone — never go out, get to know people — and just churn people from program-to-program-to-program. Who gets hurt? The little guy gets hurt.

I don't know why I give. When you're as broke as Jeannine and I were for so many years — when you have something — holy smokes, it's nice to be able to give. We feel good about giving. Money is not our God. We'd rather give it than keep it. I hope it doesn't make everybody start calling for loans. That's the one thing that's tough on us. We get calls, faxes, virtual voices, voice mail messages saying, "We need to borrow $10,000." That's what banks are for, not the upline.

The other day a lady called me. She said she was praying to God. God answered her saying I should pay off her $23,000 in credit card bills. We've had others fax notes saying, "Just sign here and send back with the money." That's the part I don't like about the money. I just don't like it at all because we are so easy going. We wish we could help the world.

There are some people who go so long without anything that when they do get something — they keep it all. But I've never heard of a funeral procession where there is a U-HAUL Trailer behind the hearse. The *money is good*. It is not evil. It's what a person *does* with the money that makes it good or evil.

I am the champion for the "little guy." It's taken me a long time to realize that *everybody* isn't going to be successful. Some people *choose* not to be successful. They don't do enough work to be successful. I've had an awful time with that because I just figure *everyone* should feel and enjoy success.

I hate to see people *not* make it. *It breaks my heart* and I get tears down my cheeks when they don't. I am the champion for the little guy, and I'm real proud of that. I've not built my business on high profile people although I do business with some. I've built my network marketing success by helping a lot of little guys — instead of a few high-profile big guys. I want to be the beacon of hope for the little guy.

I hope this is a book people will want to buy a dozen copies of and loan them out, get them back, loan them out and it will help them build their business. I don't want you to buy a book just to read about Dayle Maloney. I want you to have this book because it will help you succeed in life, build your business and touch more lives. That's why I'm doing it.

Sure, we'll make some money but guess where that money will go? To help people. I'm not proud of the book because it tells about me. I'm proud of it because I hope it *will help you* build a bigger, better business. If it helps this wonderful company grow and reach people, then we've been successful with this book, and it's all been worthwhile.

Success Secret ...

"Generosity is giving more than you can.
Pride is taking less than you need."

Nutrition For Life Distributor Spotlight ...

John and Marla Epps, 2-Star Platinum Executives with their two vehicles paid for by Nutrition For Life International.

"Dayle Maloney has always gone out of his way to help. Dayle appeals to a great number of people because most people can see a bit of themselves in Dayle."

— John & Marla Epps, Colorado
2-Star Platinum Executives

Chapter 4

Chapter 4

Those Who Laugh - Last

PART 1

A Year From Now
You May Wish
You Had Started Today

People say to me, "Dayle, I wish I had started when you did back in 1985. Dayle, if I could only start where you are now."

I didn't start here. I started at the beginning. The same place everyone starts. I say be *thankful* you *did not* get involved back in 1985 because you probably wouldn't be here today. Odds say you would have been a casualty.

Let me explain something to you. I got involved in the network marketing industry in 1983. Dale Brunner and I got involved together in Nutrition For Life in 1985. I didn't know anything about a "system of duplication." Between

1983 and 1989, I personally enrolled 2,500 people into the business. *Personally enrolled 2,500 people!* But read closely. Because we didn't have a system of duplication back then, I couldn't get a bonus check to stay above $10,000 a month — bringing in 2,500 people.

You know why? There was no system. *I was not being duplicated.* How did I finally make the kind of money I am now? Companies in the network marketing industry are realizing that their people will only succeed if those people know exactly what to do in a simple, easy way that can be duplicated. Nutrition for Life's system can be duplicated by the smallest mom-'n-pop in your organization. Only when everyone can achieve, can everyone succeed. Nutrition For Life and most importantly, Kevin Trudeau, have implemented that system.

Back in those days, without a system, we worked hard —as hard as you could work. Fourteen hours a day, 6 days a week. It took me two years to get a bonus check to stay above $2,000 a month! It took three years to get a check to stay above *$5,000 a month.*

In 1985 Dale Brunner and I had a dream. We dreamed that somehow we would become *financially independent.* We joined the program June 11, 1985, my birthday. We had a dream that we could make-it-to-the-top in network marketing. Now, in those days we sold $12 "lottery tickets." If you got involved it was $12. You didn't have to buy any product if you didn't want to. What do you suppose people did? They didn't buy any product! But if they did, we got them all to buy what we called a "$70 Starter Variety Pack." We couldn't tell you what you were going to get. Whatever wasn't selling you were going to get in that brown box when it came.

Oh, they'd get excited. They'd call me, "We haven't got our starter pack yet."

"Oh, it will be coming any day now," I'd assure them.

One spouse would tell the other, "If the package comes today, don't open it until I get home; then the family can all open it together." Well, you ought to see what was in that brown box. There was usually a purple aloe vera lipstick. There was a green aloe vera lipstick. There were about four little bottles of Elegant Cosmetics and a couple little round jars called White Gold and Black Gold with no instructions. You also received some black and white brochures.

I had gout the day I joined this program. I could hardly walk. So I bought the Variety Pack. I had heard one of those little round jars was aloe vera which might be good for gout. I didn't know if it was the white gold or the black gold. I figured I had a 50/50 chance. I bet it was the black gold. I had my whole leg looking like a blacktop driveway from rubbing on black gold for two days. Nothing helped.

I called Jana Mitcham, "I don't think your products work. I've been using the black gold for my gout."

"No, Dayle, not the black gold try the white gold," she recommended. We didn't know what to do back then.

Folks, those were tough days. People say to me everyday, "You guys — you and Brunner — were *so lucky*."

Hey, *you* are the ones that are *lucky* that you *didn't* get *involved* with us in 1985. You are the ones that are lucky. Hey, it was tough.

I would go wherever I could get an audience. One

Monday morning at 2:30 a.m. in my old junker, another distributor and I left Eau Claire heading non-stop for our first meeting that night with six people in Louisville, Kentucky. The next non-stop meeting was in Memphis, Tennessee. Next Montgomery, Alabama. Next night Tampa, Florida. Then a short hop to Jacksonville, Florida. Charleston, South Carolina. Each night a different place. Greenville, South Carolina. Winston-Salem, North Carolina. Raleigh, North Carolina. Richmond, Virginia. Washington, DC. South Jersey. North Jersey. Providence Rhode Island and then turn around and head home.

We slept two or three hours in between stops in the car. If I had twenty people it was a massive crowd. In those days, I was just trying to find anybody to talk to. Network marketing was not as widely accepted as it is today.

At the meetings I tried to get them all to, *"Please buy a little Variety Pack"* Understand, folks, in two years — because it was $12 ... a lottery ticket — over 100,000 people joined nationwide. Today probably *less than 200* of those 100,000 are still in the business. People kept dropping out and eventually it didn't work as well as we had hoped. I was a good recruiter, but because there was no system for people to run on, I found myself basically with a sales job with no security, little pay and no future for residual income. Friend, I couldn't be where I am today without the <u>system of duplication</u>. Thank you, Kevin Trudeau.

So do you think *we* were lucky back then, or are *you* lucky today? I ask, would *you* have been one of the 200 who stuck around until today? The odds say not. Those were tough days.

Today people become Nutrition For Life distributors and open their businesses — working from home — using

Nutrition For Life's simple system of success that can be duplicated. The secret of success in network marketing is duplication. To make good money you have to be with a company that has a system of duplication. All distributors in your entire organization use the exact steps you use to sponsor people as distributors in the business. Nutrition For Life and Kevin Trudeau have developed business-building techniques that are available to all of us which we can use over and over and over and are the closest thing to a guarantee of success that I've ever seen in business. The keys to the system are the books, tapes and functions. I don't believe you can succeed without them.

Don't hate yourself for missing this opportunity. Everything you need to succeed is available to you. Right now is the best time to get started in Nutrition For Life!

Mr. Meant-To

Mr. Meant-To has a comrade,
And his name is Didn't-Do.
Have you ever chanced to meet them?
Have they ever called on you?
These two fellows live together
In the house of Never-Win,
And I'm told that it is haunted
By the ghost of Might-Have-Been.

— Anonymous

PART 2

Yesterday's Dream Is Today's Hope And Tomorrow's Reality

Back in March 1989, David Bertrand and Jana Mitcham and Consumer Express acquired a little network marketing company called Nutrition For Life. David and Jana said, "We'll give ourselves at least five years and work relentlessly to get this company really ready to roll."

I'll always remember the first kick-off meetings after the acquisition. It was March 1, 1989. We went out into the field a month ahead of time. David and Jana said, "Dayle, you pick out the stops."

The first night of the first week was Mankato, Minnesota. We had 200 chairs and a terrible winter storm. You couldn't see the roads outside: sleet, ice, snow. We had 70 people show up.

The next night in Willmar, Minnesota. It was 50 degrees below zero Fahrenheit with the wind-chill. I guess we had 25 there. One guy had an accident on the way, hurt his ribs and still came to the meeting just to hear what was going on. His name was Calvin Plumley and he is a successful distributor today.

Next night Menahga, Minnesota. Why we were in Menahga, I'll never know to this day. It was 81 degrees below zero. Bertrand asked, "Do you know what you're doing, Dayle?"

I assured him, "Hey, it's just bad weather, David, next week we're going to do'er."

We all went home for the weekend and Monday night I flew out to meet David Bertrand and Jana Mitcham in Great Falls, Montana. We had 11 people in a blizzard in Great Falls. (Dave and Gail Campbell, Dr. David Biegel, and Drs. Rogers — we could have used you that night in 1989.)

The next night in Spokane, Washington we had another blizzard. The blizzard just kept following us around. It should have gone east but it seemed to be going west.

The third night was Reno, Nevada. I don't know what we were doing there yet. But the next night was my night to shine — Rexburg, Idaho. Everyone asked, "Why are we going to *Rexburg, Idaho*?

I said, "You'll see, it's going to be *gigantic*." We had to fly from Reno, Nevada, to Salt Lake City and change planes to fly to Idaho Falls, Idaho.

"Is this where it is?" inquired David when we landed.

"No, we've got to get a rental car now," I informed him.

"Really?" David questioned as he summed up the situation.

Once we were in the car, he was like a little kid. About every 10 miles he'd ask, "Are we about there? Are we about there?"

When we found Rexburg, Idaho, I said, "David, don't worry. They'll be out *big time* tonight." We found Reck's College in Rexburg and we couldn't park within 6 blocks. I said, "Now you understand why we're in Rexburg, Idaho?"

"Yah, yah, yah," David exclaimed.

We had a *3,000 seat* auditorium — big red velvet stage curtains —it was a beauty. Including the three of us, there were 11 people at the meeting in Rexburg. What happened was, the semi-finals of the state girls basketball tournament were being held across campus in the Field House. But we didn't quit. It would have been easy to give it up. Don't ever learn how to quit; learn how to keep going! You couldn't have made us quit.

The next night we were in Denver, Colorado — not much. Saturday morning we were going on to Orange County, California to be with Marjorie and Jim Llewellyn.

We were at the Denver airport waiting to catch a Continental Airlines non-stop from Denver to Orange County. The stewardess kept looking at me all the time. "What's going on?" I wondered nervously.

I was sitting with David and Jana. The stewardess came over to me and said, "Tip, you haven't flown with me for a long time. You're coming with me." First Class — she thought I was Tip O'Neill! Gosh, she got me orange juice and *smoked almonds.* Pretty soon they called the coach passengers. There went Bertrand and Mitcham, headed to the back of the plane.

We had a pretty good crowd in Orange County. We went out to eat afterwards with Marjorie Llewellyn who today is one of our top people in Nutrition For Life. But back then at the dinner table, she informed me she was quitting. My heart sank for a moment, then I decided I wasn't going to *let her* quit.

We did a meeting a few months later in Eau Claire and Marjorie wouldn't come back — but I knew Marjorie. I sent her a round trip airline ticket — Orange County to Eau Claire. I wrote in big letters, "NON-REFUNDABLE!"

I called her on the phone, "Marjorie, there's a ticket coming to you Fed Ex."

She turned to her husband, "Jim, what am I supposed to do with a ticket? He can't get his money back."

"Well, Marjorie," Jim consoled her, "at least use the ticket and take a look."

When she came back to Eau Claire we had the *red carpet out,* and she's been with us ever since. Folks, those were tough, tough days, let me tell you but we had the dream — we had the burn.

I *never* ask a prospect for a resume. I don't care were they've *been.* I care where they *want to go.* I want to know if they have *a dream.* The *dream is where it's at* in this business.

Success Secret ...

> "Use your last waking thoughts each
> night to *believe* three *impossible*
> things you want — to be true."

Nutrition For Life Distributor Spotlight ...

Jim & Marjorie Llewellyn

"My husband, Jim, will be 80 this September. Together, we own L&H Nutrition in Fullerton, California. He and I began studying nutrition 25 years ago because of my health. Our strength is product knowledge rather than concentrating on working the business opportunity, and the money has always come for us. Once people begin to use the product, they like it and use it forever. We have been one of the top three retailers in Nutrition For Life year after year. Jim helped develop Oraflow Plus and because we sell so much. I'm known around the country as Mrs. Oraflow Plus. Today our family drives 3 cars which are all paid for by Nutrition For Life."

— Marjorie and Jim Llewellyn, California
Platinum Executives

PART 3

Leadership By Example

Jana Mitcham, Co-Founder and Executive Vice-President, Nutrition For Life, Houston, Texas
Leadership Means You Have The Authority
To Serve People In A Special Way

Dayle Maloney has built his network marketing business brick-by-brick, helping and motivating many people to each contribute a little towards the success of the entire organization. Because of the enormous amount of care he has for others, I have watched Dayle's checks increase faster than anybody we've had in our company to date.

Watching Dayle's generosity, I would have never guessed how close he was to financial disaster. Two years into our relationship, I discovered how bad his situation really was. Many of the people Dayle helped during those times were actually better off than he was, but he helped them anyway. Dayle's philosophy has always been, "If I'm making it, it's because my downline is helping me. What's mine is theirs."

Nutrition For Life's President, David Bertrand, and I counsel Dayle: "You have to be cautious."

There are people who have taken advantage of Dayle's big heart and we try to protect him. We have the same concern for *all* our distributors.

New distributors call me and say, "Wow! I got *you* on the telephone?"

I gently laugh as I ask, "Why wouldn't you get *me* on the telephone? I'm working for *you*."

The lines of communication are open between the corporate office and the field. David and I believe we must be in constant communication with our distributors. We work Monday through Friday at the corporate office. Friday afternoon we hop a plane to a meeting or event and come home Sunday just in time for church with our families.

I feel David and I set the tone for the belief level in the field. I care very deeply for people and want everyone to succeed. Relationships with people are held very dear to my heart. Being a heartfelt person, tears come very easily to me. One of my greatest challenges is to make it through a situation where I feel someone has wronged another without tears filling my eyes. Some people may see that as a weakness. Nonsense. I am proof that real people with caring hearts succeed.

Through many years of hard work and cultivating caring relationships, I have been blessed with a wonderful life. My philosophy is, "If God has given me something, it belongs to everybody." I'll be out of town and the church or the youth group will use my house or my car.

Network marketing is a blessing and the only future for people who want to control their destiny. The first step is to choose to be involved with folks you believe in.

It's important for people to know what David and I stand for as the management of Nutrition For Life. When David and I are at a meeting or event we ask people to listen to us, watch us, and look at the group of leaders we've assembled. At the end of the meeting, people need to decide, "Do I like them, trust them, and do I want to do business with them?"

Jana Mitcham at the Captain's Table with Nutrition For Life leaders: (l to r) Tom Schreiter, Dr. Tom Klesmit, Judy Bertrand, David Bertrand, Kevin Trudeau, Jana Mitcham, Captain, Dayle Maloney, Jeannine Maloney, Wes Speigel, Jane Speigel, Sue Schreiter

Success Secret ...

"Take away our people and leave our building, and soon dust will collect on the switchboard. Take away our building and leave our people, and soon we will have a new and better building."

PART 4

When You Help Others You Better Yourself

David & Gail Campbell,
3-Star Platinum Executives , Montana
Making Friends Is The Key To Success

Gail and I are seeing that Nutrition For Life attracts people who care about other people. We think that anybody who is a quality person can not help but finish first in Nutrition For Life because of the opportunity, the company and the products. Nutrition For Life is all about caring and really provides the stage for *nice people* to *finish first.*

In fact, we think if a person is not a "good guy" he or she would have a hard time succeeding. The secret to success in this business is to help others get what they want — be that better health, personal self-image, financial stability, independence, or the security that forever comes from a strong circle of dedicated friends.

What's the message we've learned from Dayle and now live by? When you help enough people get what they want, you can not help but be rewarded in numerous ways for many, many years to come.

In network marketing your wealth is measured by more than just your money. It's measured in terms of the friends that you've made and the connections you have with these great, classy, go-to-it-and-do-it, caring people.

In the last 2 ½ years we've met more super-super people than in all the years we've operated our other businesses. If you're tired of "putting up with people" and wonder where to find good people to do business with ... you'll find them in Nutrition for Life.

I was a stockbroker, realtor, insurance agent and still hold a CPA license. Gail and I have owned successful companies in all fields. I want you to know Gail and I looked at a lot of business opportunities and this is the single finest business opportunity we've ever seen for the average person to <u>change</u> <u>their</u> <u>life</u> <u>forever</u>.

If you're building this business, it doesn't seem to make a difference whether you're in Dayle's downline or not — he works with you either way. Dayle came out and held a seminar for us. Then later that summer he flew Gail and me, all expenses paid, to Eau Claire where I did a meeting for his downline. A month later, he flew us to Saskatoon and Eau Claire again.

That really promoted and helped us in the company. Here's a guy who really loves network marketing and he's willing to open arms and share his vision, enthusiasm and success.

My favorite statement is, "That old white-haired guy is the smartest one of all." He is. He makes everyone feel like family. As long as you're going to work the business — he'll do anything he can for you. The people in Montana just love him. We had the first Montana Nutrition for Life Picnic. Dayle always talks about no-shows. Well, at this picnic *everybody showed up*! In fact we planned for 300 people and 500 showed. We couldn't feed them all.

This year, at the 2nd annual picnic, I think we'll have 1,200 people there. It's because Dayle just gets in and helps. We call our annual picnic "The Dayle Maloney Picnic Where Everybody Shows Up."

If Dayle lost all his money tomorrow — he'd still be one of the richest men in America. Any of us could lose *all* our money. With the friends and connections we've made in this business, we're confident we would have it back in no time.

The people who are the most successful in this business are those who build lasting, long-term relationships.

How do people build those relationships? First, you *don't* need to be outgoing! In fact, Dayle Maloney was *so shy* he couldn't even raise his hand in school. Although he never graduated, Dayle did attend some college. He dropped out of speech class when he was told the next day he would have to get up in front of the room and talk. *He couldn't do it* — he got sick and couldn't go to class. <u>Dayle Maloney was SHY</u>!

So if an introverted, shy guy can build lasting friendships — become so popular — what's the secret? <u>A belief in helping fellow men and women</u>.

Dave & Gail Campbell
3-Star Platinum Executives, Montana

Success Secret ...

"If you're in a situation where you are
wondering what to do, ask yourself,
'What would Dayle Maloney do?'
Then do that."

PART 5

Cure Fear
and Build Confidence

Bill & Sherri Tucker,
Platinum Executives, Washington
Practice Doing What Your Heart Tells You Is Right

Forty-five years old and at the lowest point of my life, Sherri and I started our Nutrition For Life business. I was grasping at straws when I agreed to join. I just didn't have it in my heart to build an organization because of what we went through with another network marketing company.

Being raised by an alcoholic father, I grew up believing I could not be successful. My dad found fault in everything. I tried desperately to win his approval — even to the point of becoming an alcoholic myself.

Our network marketing business has not been easy for Sherri and me to build. When Sherri and I started in March of 1992, we didn't have a lot of money but we listened to Dayle's audio tape messages repeating, "Hang in there. Don't ever learn how to quit."

There was a time Sherri and I became real discouraged because we showed the plan to 80 people who said, "No." Today, we can see many of the no's were because we just didn't believe in ourselves. We believed in the products, the company, and all of the other people who were doing it — but we had a hard time believing we could succeed.

We shared our discouragement with our upline sponsor and less than 2 hours later, Dayle called us. Right after Dayle, Kevin Trudeau called. These calls gave us the will to stick with it. Without Dayle's influence in our lives — we wouldn't be in NFL today. Dayle has taught us how to relate to people on a business plane as well as on a personal level.

I sat with Dayle for lunch and he said, "Bill, this business can be built as big as you want! The number one thing that will help you build it is to *be yourself.* You are a guy that *loves people* — let that be your strong suit. Don't get sucked in with all those hot-shots who come along and go-to-the-top, really fast. They are here today — sometimes gone tomorrow. Just be yourself, love your people, be there for them, and you will be successful."

I agreed to follow Dayle's advice because he practices what he preaches. Dayle knows people count on him, and he will not let them down. He will be there for his people even when he's exhausted. That is the kind of leader I will become.

Dayle says, "You aren't born a leader and we can't teach you to be a leader. You are developed as a leader which is a process."

Recognizing we had a long ways to go personally, this business afforded us the atmosphere to grow. We surround ourselves with people like Dayle Maloney, Dale Brunner, Jim Leyde, David Bertrand and Jana Mitcham, Jim Horn, and other many wonderful people who are leaders in Nutrition For Life.

Sherri and I have built this business slowly because we have had a long journey with our own personal growth. My message will touch the hearts of those folks like us who don't seem to have a lot of charisma and don't seem to have a lot going for them. We were not "super people" who achieved Platinum status in 6 months and become a 4-Star Platinum in 2 years. We have achieved the success of being Platinum today because we are people who stuck with it! With the same persistence, we will become 4-Star Platinums.

When I reach the point that I am speaking on stage, I will relate, "It is a process, and don't give up on the process." My message will ring in the hearts of people who are sick and tired of their lives — who don't want to live the way they are living. I have been there and because I am on the other side, saving one or two people makes the pain from earlier in my life of value.

Remember when Sherri and I showed the plan to 80 people and they all said, "No"? One of the reasons we didn't believe in ourselves was because we were trying to believe in someone else's dream. We thought we had to force dreams of a big house, expensive car — you know, "lifestyles of the rich and famous" dreams? Those didn't work for us. We enjoyed the "idea" of those things, but they didn't make the flame of passion burn inside us. Our dream was simply to help people.

When the dream stealers begin to pour the venom on, I go through self talk and say, "They don't see my goal. They don't understand the direction I am going, but I do. I am going to continue in that direction because it is worthwhile, honorable, and it reflects the value system I have deep in my heart that needs to be guarded."

The dreams we have now have been deep within us all the time, but we didn't know it. With the help of Dayle and

Nutrition For Life's training, the Master Developer Series, we were able to place a finger on our dreams, understand what they were and where they were going to take us. This has only taken place within the last 9-12 months.

Dayle is the father of this organization. Dayle believes in me and I love him for it. I didn't have a father to do that. The next time I see him I have to say, "Dayle, I can't thank you enough."

I am proud to be part of the company, proud to be affiliated with Dayle Maloney and proud to be in his downline. There is no other company I would ever join because of Nutrition For Life's integrity.

Bill & Sherri Tucker, Platinum Executives, Washington

Success Secret ...

"When you help one person, that person will touch another — like a skipping stone tossed into a pond, the ripple effect will begin."

PART 6

You Can Succeed In Anything For Which You Have Enthusiasm

What are the ten success ingredients you need to build a big business in Nutrition For Life? I'll reveal the 10 key things *all* successful people have. Are you ready? Number one is ... the dream. Number two is ... the dream. Number three is the dream, four a dream, five a dream, six a dream, seven a dream, eight a dream, nine a dream and number ten is a dream! That is what you need to build this business. Dream, dream, dream! Believe in your dream!

When you believe in your dream with excitement, you can't help but build a business. The only people that aren't excited are the folks that look like they've been weaned on a *dill pickle*! You have to laugh. You've got to get *excited*. You can't hold that laughter in. If you try to it's going to come out your thighs ... so let 'er go. Let 'er rip.

Those who laugh, last ... Absolutely true. When you're excited and you meet those prospects, give them a good handshake. Now if their whole body starts to tremble, you're shaking too hard. Look them in the eye and shake their hand. Turn your lights on and let them know somebody is home. That's part of a solid handshake.

And talk about being excited … it makes me think of little Nathan Madison from Oxnard, California. I promised Nathan if he and his parents ever came to visit me here in Wisconsin, I would make sure he got to go fishing on the dock down the hill from my house at the lake.

Nathan and his parents arrived in August, a few days before the Nutrition For Life National Convention. It was a rainy summer night, and they had driven non-stop from Los Angeles. We didn't fish that night. Monday everyone was busy — no chance to fish. Wednesday they were going to go on to Minneapolis for the convention, so Tuesday was the last chance to fish. Lo and behold, I had to hold a meeting in Thorp, Wisconsin, with Peter Angell and Nathan's father Wydell.

I said, "Nathan, I don't know if we're going to have a chance to fish." I saw the tears streaming down his cheeks. I said, "Hey, I can't do this to him!" I called my brother-in-law and said, "Dallas come on up here — you've just got to help me out — and take little Nathan to the dock to get some fish."

Dallas is a good man. He said, "Yep, I'll be right up." So I told Nathan's dad, "Wydell, my brother-in-law is coming up here and he's going to take Nathan down on the dock to get some fish."

"No, the boy can't swim, the boy can't swim. I just don't want him down there." Wydell insisted.

"Oh, listen, Wydell. My brother-in-law is a good man and will be with Nathan the whole time. You don't have to worry about a thing." I begged for Nathan's sake.

"No, I don't think the boy ought to do it." Wydell said firmly.

"Well, Wydell, Dallas is already on his way up here." I contested.

Wydell agreed. Peter Angell, Wydell and I went out, did the meeting and came back to the house. Loretta, Wydell's wife, took me to the side and whispered, "Dayle, you won't believe this. We don't want Wydell to know about it. When Nathan caught that first fish, he got so excited, he went *off the dock backwards*." Dallas did a quick scoop-out-of-the-lake, saving Nathan and his prize catch!

I'd call that a two for one offer. Nathan got to go fishing and swimming all in the same trip.

Success Secret ...

"People who find the fire of
excitement within their hearts excel."

Nutrition For Life Distributor Spotlight ...

Nathan Madison and his fish

Nathan, Loretta, Wydell, and Torsheda Madison

"We have been in five networking marketing companies and have been hurt in all of them except for Nutrition For Life. The only network marketing company where we have made money is Nutrition For Life, and we are in for life."

—Wydell and Loretta Madison
1-Star Platinum Executives, California

PART 7

Only Love
Can Awaken Love

Tara and Tracy Ternberg,
Platinum Executives, Wisconsin
What Is It Like To Be Related To
Dayle And Jeannine Maloney?

Growing up I was Tara, Dayle's little Zelder Bug.
When I was little, I never knew Uncle Dayle was broke or
how deep in debt he was. At Christmas time, he always had
garbage bags full of toys. He'd take my friends and me
shopping and buy us all Barbies. I'm probably part of why he
was so much in debt — all the toys he bought me.

When I was in school, every year he'd throw a
birthday party for me with 10 of my friends. He'd take us
roller skating and then to a pizza party. Dayle was generous
before he had money. Through his willingness to always be
my friend, he has taught me a great deal and shown me how
wonderful life is.

Everywhere Dayle traveled, he'd send me a postcard.
I had stacks and stacks of postcards. He'd write: "Hugs and

kisses, Love, Uncie." He's close to our entire family, but I think because I am his first niece, we have a special bond.

The first time my husband, Tracy, met Dayle and Jeannine was 9½ years ago when we were dating and we asked to borrow their car for high school prom. Dayle and Jeannine didn't know Tracy, who was 16 years old at the time, but they loaned him their Chrysler New Yorker. It's hard for people to imagine how they could lend their car to someone they didn't know — especially a teenage boy. Even today, material possessions mean nothing to Jeannine and Dayle but giving people the opportunity to experience the pleasures of life with dignity means everything.

Jeannine and Dayle don't spend a dime on themselves. Dayle, Tracy and I were up in Alaska with the Nutrition For Life *Mind and Body Institute* and had a few extra hours to see a glacier. While there, we stopped at the little gift shop. "This is the nicest little souvenir shop," Dayle commented which is unusual because Dayle doesn't like shopping. A wolf figurine caught his attention. It was about $400 — which isn't much money for someone who earns what Dayle does. I think he felt guilty at the idea of spending money on himself, so we coaxed him until he bought it: "Dayle, you deserve it! Spend some money on yourself." He'd rather use the money to help others.

Dayle and Jeannine donated somewhere around $400,000 to build our hometown church. Originally, the congregation intended on treating the money as a loan. Tracy and I attended a church meeting where members of the congregation were developing a payment plan. Dayle and Jeannine listened quietly. Pastor Johnson recommended to the group that the congregation repay $2000 a month. Dayle leaned forward and said, "Well, Jeannine and I *donated* that money and truly don't expect to get paid back."

We're talking more than $400,000! About forty-five congregation members were present. Except for Tracy, Jeannine, Dayle and me— everyone was shocked and sat in disbelief for several minutes. Here the congregation thought the $400,000 was a loan. They couldn't believe anyone would really be so generous as to donate *that* kind of money. Applause filled the room. Imagine the congregation's relief when we opened the church debt free!

Dayle and Jeannine's generosity and their trust that God will always take care of them are the building blocks to their success. When he first started, Dayle was an unknown "nobody." He had a powerful love in his heart that most people don't have. Dayle lives by the philosophy of the more he gives, the more he will receive. It doesn't mean those who Dayle takes care of, will be those who are able to give back.

Dayle and Jeannine feed the possums who live in the woods surrounding their home. When we go out of town together, they find someone to go over to their house *every* night and make sure the possums are fed. In Dayle's heart he firmly believes those possums can't go without food. Tracy tells him, "They are wild animals. They're used to surviving a day without food." But Dayle insists on taking care of them. Maybe it's because Dayle lived with the pain of going without as a kid and wants to rid the world of suffering.

The neighbors had a tame goose and duck that lived in their yard, and Dayle was *so* concerned those birds were going to get hit. My parents had a pheasant who ate from their bird feeder. It was hit on the road right outside their house. To this day, Dayle sadly admits, "I can't drive by that spot without thinking about that poor pheasant." Dayle's concern about *all* living creatures comes from deep in his soul, and his heart aches when others are hurting.

No matter how much pain, Dayle believes: "Never learn how to quit." He's not just saying that because thousands of people are watching him and it's what they expect him to say. Dayle actually believes you should never quit! Dayle never quits — no matter what the price.

His mind is always on the business. Jeannine and I will be talking, and Dayle will cut in and ask, "So, Tara, did you get that inventory taken?"

Jeannine already knows the answer, but she has to ask, "Dayle, can't you ever think about anything but business?"

Some may think Dayle is a workaholic, but we don't think so. We think he's a "people-aholic." Tracy and I have traveled all over with him and have never heard him say a bad word about anybody. Dayle gets fired up, don't get us wrong, but he just doesn't get vicious or hold a grudge. People have taken advantage of his willingness to help. For example, after Dayle has helped people develop their talents, they leave for another company. Dayle will still have lunch with them and be good-hearted. He tells us, "Tracy and Tara, you never want to burn a bridge. Others can make the mistake and burn the bridge, but you always leave enough bridge for them to walk back across it and rebuild."

Dayle, Tara and Tracy
enjoying time together at a glacier in Alaska

Success Secret ...

"Practice random kindness and
senseless acts of beauty."

PART 8

Thank You For Being My Friend

Mitch and Nan Walter, Gold Executives, Montana
Do You Want To Know What A Person Is Made Of?
Ask A Child

At this point in his life, Dayle could choose to spend his life on the beaches of the world. Instead, he goes out and personally meets with the people, helping them enhance their lives.

Dayle came to our home after the famous *Montana Dayle Maloney Picnic Where Everybody Showed Up*. Our son, David, who is 4 years old now but who was three at the time, wanted to play basketball after supper. Dayle had a full day of speaking in front of 450 people and hours of meetings. He was tired like anyone would be after being the main speaker and the focus of hundreds of people's attention.

But David really wanted to play ball with Dayle, his new found friend. We told David that Dayle was too tired.

Dayle wouldn't have any of that. He rose out of his chair and took David by the hand proceeding to play basketball.

Dayle made a hoop out of his arms in front of his body, and David threw the basketball into the hoop. According to 3-year old David, Dayle wasn't locking his fingers exactly right or making the arm hoop big enough. Three-year old David instructed Dayle exactly how to lock his fingers and make the hoop as big as possible. Dayle followed David's directions. David proceeded to bounce the basketball off Dayle's stomach and into the hoop for about 30 minutes.

Even though Dayle was exhausted, he took the time to care and listen to a child. As I tell you this story, David is jumping up and down next to me, his eyes sparkling with excitement and love as he locks his fingers saying, "Make a hoop, Dayle. Make a hoop."

When David grows up he will realize exactly who his special friend is. Imagine the impact on David when he learns that one of the great men of our century spent time with him when he was just 3 years old: "When I was just a little one, that man saw something special in me and spent his time as my friend."

Success Secret ...

"A person never stands as tall as when he or she kneels to help a child."

Dayle and David playing "hoop" in Montana.

**The Montana Dayle Maloney Picnic
Where Everybody Showed Up**

PART 9

The Only Real Training For Leadership is Leadership

Families are important. Jeannine and I have members of her family working over at the Eau Claire Nutrition For Life Distribution Center. Jeannine's sister, Kathy, and her husband, Dallas Swanstrom, both help us out over there. This business has been good for our family and many others. Our niece, Tara Ternberg, and her husband, Tracy, both work full-time managing our office. Our nephew, Dana, and our niece, Tessa, are both students but also work part-time in the office.

In 1993, Dallas and Kathy hosted a foreign exchange student from Sofia, Bulgaria. His name was Peter Dossov. Peter attended Mondovi High School. I remember seeing leadership in this guy. I loved this kid.

I told him for his high school graduation I would take him to all the World Cup Soccer Games where Bulgaria played. The 1994 World Cup was in the United States. Bulgaria, Peter's homeland, had a previous World Cup record of zero wins and 16 losses or ties.

Every team that makes the World Cup plays three games during the qualifying round.

The first game in Texas, Dallas went with Peter to

watch Bulgaria play Nigeria. Nigeria won. The second game was in Chicago. I made it to that one. Bulgaria beat Greece 4-0. Third game — and the last game of the qualifying round — was back in Texas. Dallas took Peter. Lo and behold, Bulgaria upset Argentina, which meant they continued to the next round! The next game was July 5, 1994 in New Jersey. It was Bulgaria against Mexico in Meadowlands Stadium.

Peter and I flew out for the game. I'm conditioning Peter because now just one loss and his team is out. I said, "Peter, your country has done well but it's a long shot that you can beat Mexico."

"Oh, we win," Peter said with his accent, "we will win."

I watched in awe as they beat Mexico in a shoot-out 2-1.

We flew back home. The next game was against Germany, defending World Cup Champions. By all odds, Bulgaria didn't have a chance against those Germans — but back we went to New Jersey. Dallas, Peter, Dana and Tracy Ternberg drove my van out to the game. I finished business and flew out the night before the game. Everyone knew Bulgaria was going to be defeated by Germany — everyone except Peter.

It was probably the greatest single sporting event I've ever seen — and I've been to a lot of them. Germany was ahead 1-0. It looked bad for Bulgaria. In the second half Hristo Stoichkov, who is the best Bulgarian player — *the man* of Bulgaria — delivered a free kick in to the net — it was like a bullet — it curved around the goalie and tied the game 1-1. A short time later Bulgaria got a header for a second goal. *They upset Germany 2-1.*

I flew to Puerto Rico for two days of meetings leaving the guys out in New York. Then I flew back to New Jersey for Bulgaria versus Italy in the semi-finals. Italy beat Bulgaria 2-1.

What impressed me most about Peter was his leadership abilities. Here's a kid — 17 years old — over here in a foreign country. There were only about 100 Bulgarian fans at any of the games. We would arrive at the games about 2 hours early. Peter would identify his countrymen by the big capes and hats with the Bulgaria team colors. I don't know how he ever got away with it, but he would sit at about the 50 yard line in the middle of the group.

Peter was their cheerleader. There was an old guy from Bulgaria that was always there. He was the drummer while Peter would lead the cheers. Peter would wear his big cape and hat, and it would blow in the wind. I sat and observed in admiration.

The funniest of all was after each game, we would have an agreed upon spot where we would meet. I would say, "Peter, when you're all done celebrating with your fellow Bulgarians here's where we'll meet to leave."

"Yep," He'd always say to me.

So Bulgaria upset Germany 2-1 — when they weren't supposed to have a chance. We were waiting for Peter at the meeting spot. Pretty soon we hear, "Boom. Boom. Boom." It was the drum. We turned our heads towards the sound and here came 100 Bulgarians marching in formation with this drummer. Who do you suppose was leading the parade? *Peter!* He was marching out in front wearing his cape, hat and head held high with great pride.

I shouted, "Peter! Where ya' goin'?"

He replied loudly, "We're marching to the team bus."

Using as much voice as I had left, I replied, "Where *is* it?"

"We don't know ..." He said out of reflex, and they just kept right on going.

I'll never forget that as long as I live. It's one of the highlights of my life, watching Peter lead the marching group to the bus having no idea where it was to be found.

That night I left for Puerto Rico and the guys stayed. The Bulgarian team invited Peter and a few of the leaders to come out to a little hotel in New Jersey and join the team for their victory party. Here's a kid that's 17 years old, over here in America and gets invited to the victory party. A huge honor. Dallas, Dana and Tracy took Peter out to the hotel.

By the next day, Peter had in his hands pictures of all the Bulgarian world cup players and autographed soccer balls. Can you imagine the feeling the young fellow had?

Two days later, when he was ready to go back to Bulgaria, I couldn't stand to see the guy leave. I had a hard time fighting the tears. That Monday, we had him fly from Eau Claire to Minneapolis, then Minneapolis to New York. I had a limousine driver take him from LaGuardia Airport in New York to JFK Airport for the Balkan Airline Flight to Bulgaria.

Peter arrived in New York and they announced the flight to Sofia was going to be delayed four hours. What had really happened was that the Bulgarian soccer team had to play a consolation game. The plane was delayed waiting for the soccer team.

You can imagine what happened when the soccer team arrived, all the big heroes getting all the first class seats, and then spotting Peter. Peter is *their man* again! He got all his pictures from the party autographed.

Can you imagine the thrill? Soccer in Bulgaria is like football here. These were Bulgaria's Superbowl winners!

When Kathy and Dallas' daughter, Tara, and Tracy Ternberg got married in 1996, Jeannine and I flew Peter back for the wedding. I told him if he would come to America and go to college, we would put him through college and it wouldn't cost him 5 cents.

August, 1997, Peter returned and is now a marketing student at the University of Wisconsin - Eau Claire. You'll meet him at the conventions and big rallies. I'm very proud of Peter Dossov.

Success Secret ...

"The second you commit and stop holding back, doors will open, people will help, material goods will appear, coincidence will happen ... and results will favor you."

Nutrition For Life Distributor Spotlight ...

Jim and Melody Hutson
(Melody was Mrs. Missouri 1991)

"We were preparing for Melody to go to the Philippines. Dayle found out and he contacted us. He said to call if we needed any help. He gave us names and phone numbers of people in the Philippines who would help us. What's so amazing is he doesn't make any money from us because we are not even in his downline."

— Jim & Melody Hutson,
2-Star Platinum Executives, Missouri

PART 10

State Legislator Speaks On Network Marketing

Ted Mina, 2-Star Platinum Executive, Hawaii
Network Marketing Is A Credible Industry

I am a former State Legislator having served in the Hawaii House of Representatives from 1976 to 1978. After my term, I went back to my successful real estate and insurance business. In 1981, I suffered a very severe heart attack and had open heart surgery — a six coronary artery bypass. The surgery was not successful and my arteries began to close. The doctors recommended another surgery, but I refused.

Prior to the heart attack, I was a heavy smoker, drank my share of coffee and was no stranger to alcohol. Being a politician and running my business, I burned the candle at both ends.

After I became ill, I couldn't keep the business going at the same successful pace, and my wife, Geri, was not licensed in real estate or insurance. Thank God, Dayle came into my life. My primary purpose for joining Nutrition For Life was to create a residual income which, regardless if I was here or not, would pay my family forever.

Because of the product line Geri and I offered through our Nutrition For Life business, I researched homeopathy and alternative health care. It proved to be an alternative to my much needed surgery and the terrible side effects I was experiencing with the prescription medications. I concluded I might find some help with a product Nutrition For Life offered called Master Key Plus. I began to take it in 1985. Did it work?

I'm still here today with my family, full of energy and life. My good health is a miracle.

My health steadily increased as Geri and I built our Nutrition For Life business. We had numerous challenges because we were the pioneers here in Hawaii. For me, the road to success wasn't always smooth. There were plenty of times I could have easily thrown the towel in and quit this business. People would say, "Ted, you are a former legislator. Why are you doing this Mickey Mouse network marketing business? This company is not going to survive. Ted, why don't you just quit and go back to your real estate and insurance business where you were doing good?"

Why did I stay with it? I figured if Dayle could do it, I knew I could, too. He inspired me to hang in there and keep going. When people laughed at me or joined the business and quit, I said, "Next."

Because I have hung in there, I am realizing my dream: to go back and help the people of my homeland, the Philippines. Geri and I have family there and now that

Nutrition For Life is open in the Philippines we can finally live our dream and increase our peoples' health *and* wealth.

Don't let anybody steal your dreams and never, never, never quit. Dayle is living proof of the success which comes from hanging on to a dream. He is a legend and has set the example for us by leading and inspiring us to achieve our dreams. God Bless. Aloha.

Geri & Ted Mina and Family, Hawaii

Success Secret ...

"Keep away from little people who try to belittle your ambitions. Small people do that, but great people make you feel that you, too, can become great."

PART 11

Act As If What You Do Makes A Difference — It Does!

Dr. David Biegel
4-Star Platinum Executive, Montana
With Integrity, Honesty And Persistence —
Anything Is Possible

My nine year optometry practice is going strong. I opened my Nutrition For Life business in December, 1995 and my organization has been growing at a great pace since day one.

Dayle held a meeting here in Montana. It was a life changing event for me. He is a *legend* in business and *my hero* even before I met him!

Three hundred people attended. I was blown away by Dayle's humor as well as his ability to relate to an audience. Dayle Maloney has been lower than most people can imagine, and *he's just kept on going* towards his dreams! Dayle is a normal guy who is a giant. He is *proof* with integrity, honesty and persistence — <u>anything</u> <u>is</u> <u>possible</u>. The good guy or gal *does win.* Dayle has proven that.

At that meeting one of the many new distributors who signed up was a young guy just starting out. We introduced him to Dayle who must have seen the spark of something in his eyes. Before we knew it, our new distributor had about $100 worth of Dayle's business building tools that Dayle handpicked for him. What did it cost our new distributor? Nothing. It was FREE! What is most remarkable is that I am not in Dayle's downline nor is this new distributor. Dayle makes no money by helping us. Will that come back to Dayle in ways other than a downline commission? Think with your heart, and you know the answer.

My success in Nutrition For Life comes from a secret of Dayle's: **focus on the *people* and the money will come.** Care about the folks and the good you are doing for them — instead of how big your check is going to be this month. Once you focus on the distributors ... you can't spend all the money. Dayle is a tremendous example of how to succeed in any business by focusing on the people.

Dr. David Biegel
4-Star Platinum Executive, Montana

Success Secret ...

"Focus on the people and the money will come."

PART 12

Leaders Build Their Follower's Dreams

Drs. Neal & Linda Rogers,
2-Star Platinum Executives, Montana
Respect People And Help Them Reach Their Dreams

My wife, Linda, is a pediatrician who was in practice for 15 years. I am an eye, ear, nose and throat specialist. Prior to our joining Nutrition For Life, we didn't give network marketing much thought.

We feel so blessed with our success because we really just stumbled into this company. What prompted us to move forward and join Nutrition For Life was the strong nutritional product line and the business training provided by Nightingale Conant and Distributor Services, and Nutrition For Life. We had been purchasing Nightingale Conant business audio programs for years.

We immediately identified Dayle Maloney as the soul and personality of this company. President David Bertrand and Executive Vice-President Jana Mitcham are honest, solid, stable and reliable.

Dayle always has time for people. He is100% genuine and totally down-to-earth.

One of the people in our downline organization, Charlie Janz, from Eugene, Oregon, met Dayle at a function.

Afterwards, a huge group of people were in line waiting to shake Dayle's hand. When Charlie's turn in line finally came, he said, "Gosh, Dayle we would love to have you come out to Eugene Oregon and do something for us — some kind of a meeting or a product day, or whatever. We would love to have you out there!"

Dayle replied, "Okay, well, let me keep that in mind, and as soon as I can work on my schedule, I will be in touch."

Charlie didn't hear from Dayle but didn't think too much about it: "Well, it was a big crowd; it was the first time he met me, and there is no reason Dayle would remember."

Recently, a large group of Nutrition For Life distributors earned free cruises. We were on the ship in the dining room and through the crowd, from across the room, Dayle spotted Charlie. Dayle came over and said, "Charlie, I owe you a meeting and I am sorry I forgot to call you. I will call you this next week and take care of it."

Dayle did call. He and Charlie set up an event in Eugene, Oregon. Dayle came to Eugene on his own nickel and didn't get paid a cent to hold the event. We are not even in his downline, so he doesn't get paid to help us.

He has impacted us by his example, by the things he has overcome, by his caring, by his integrity, and his endless enthusiasm and energy. Dayle is proof that good-hearted people and people with challenges can succeed — just like he did in spite of the physical handicaps he struggles with. Dayle is an example of the person most people want to be remembered as.

Linda has retired from her practice to speak across the nation on the wonderful nutritional products Nutrition For

Life offers. During her three years in this business, she has positively impacted more lives than she ever did with her successful pediatric practice — mentally, physically, and financially.

Drs. Linda & Neal Rogers
2-Star Platinum Executives, Montana

Success Secret ...

"When you help two people who go out the next day and do the same, by the seventh day, 120 lives will be impacted. Twenty-one days later — 2,000,000 lives will be changed."

PART 13

Humor Heals The World

Pastor David Allbritton, 4-Star Platinum, Texas
Know A Man's Character By
What Excites His Laughter

At times Dayle Maloney's business skills can go unnoticed because of his great sense of humor. He is one of the funniest men and greatest motivational speakers I have ever heard. Every time the opportunity presents itself to hear Dayle Maloney speak, I want to be there. God gifted Dayle in human relations and public speaking.

Dayle is able to share his thoughts in a way people want to listen because as they are learning they are being entertained in a clean, family-oriented way. Recently I heard Dayle ask a large audience, "If a man speaks in the forest, and there is no woman to hear him, is he still wrong?"

Dayle is a wonderful Christian man who has a ton of determination. His actions show genuine concern for other people. We have had the privilege of praying together; he really loves the Lord. Dayle wants people to know the Lord, but he does not preach. Instead, he leads by example. He opens his heart so others can watch the Lord through Dayle's actions.

During a weekend event in San Diego, I scheduled a Bible study for those who wanted to attend. Over the course of the weekend, I heard Dayle personally invite people to come join us for the Bible study. When time for the event arrived, Dayle was the first person to walk in the room and he prayed with the group. That spoke volumes to me.

One time, Dayle and I were in Eau Claire in a snowstorm and Dayle was driving. He can't see out of one eye, and has 40% vision in the other, and I can't see out of my right eye.

Dayle looked out over the hood and asked, "Is anything coming?"

I looked over and laughed, "You're asking me? I can't see out of one eye either." We teased each other about using my good left eye and his good right eye to see where we were going. We both knew it was by the grace of God we made it home that day.

Even today when we shake hands, we have to tilt our heads so we can see each other.

I have been with Nutrition For Life 1 ½ years and am a 4-Star Platinum. I finance a good portion of my missionary work through my success with my Nutrition For Life business. I am also a member of the 4-Star Platinum board which represents the distributors in the field. I know first hand the inner-happenings of Nutrition For Life and am very impressed with how well this company takes care of its distributors.

Nutrition For Life is the greatest network marketing opportunity. Not another company out there pays this well, and the products are fantastic. We have witnessed the healing of many people in our downline from the products.

Pastor David Allbritton and family: wife, Linda and 3 children: April, 10; twins Andrew and Matthew, 8.

Success Secret ...

"A person with a sense of humor doesn't make a joke out of life, they simply recognize those that already exist."

PART 14

Don't Confuse Slight Inconveniences with Actual Problems

Colleen Foerster and Bruce Rueter,
4-Star Platinum Executives, South Dakota
Enjoy Life Knowing That Nobody's Perfect

We were attending several seminars at Dr. Morter's Healthweek. Every morning before the seminars we ate breakfast together: Dayle, Colleen and I. One morning Dayle ordered French toast and his *sausage.* He started eating the sausage and he told us, "I suppose that Dr. Morter will show up. He catches me all the time. He's always harping on me not to eat this sausage, but I just love it. I don't think Dr. Morter will be here this early today."

Sure enough, Colleen and I were facing Dayle. We looked up just as Dayle was confessing how much he loved sausage, and here came Dr. Morter up behind him. We didn't even have time to warn Dayle. Dr. Morter placed his hands on Dayle's shoulders, looked at the fork full of sausage about to go in Dayle's mouth and asked sternly, "How's your sausage this morning, Dayle?" We couldn't keep from laughing.

Dayle looked at us like a housecat caught with a parakeet in its mouth. When Dr. Morter walked away, Dayle was feeling guilty because he was at *Healthweek* being presented by one of his personal physicians and was caught eating this *greasy sausage*. Dayle said, 'I'll get that Dr. Morter. Tomorrow morning I'll order room service — knowing *my luck* he'll be the one delivering it!"

Dayle didn't order sausage for the rest of the week. He's so funny. We just love that guy. There's no one else like him.

We're not sure if a few days without sausage helped Dayle's health or not, but it sure helped his stress level not to have to worry about getting caught.

Bruce Rueter and Colleen Foerster
4-Star Platinum Executives, South Dakota

Success Secret ...

"Focus 90% of your time on solutions and only 10% of your time on problems."

PART 15

Listen To Good Advice

Joanne Sokoloski,
1-Star Platinum Executive, Canada
Do You Want Better Results?

In most network marketing companies, less than 20% of the distributors attend the major functions. I'll tell you something, as far as I'm concerned those other 80% are still just *prospects.* They don't know what we learn at the functions. They're only prospects.

Now, maybe you haven't been invited to a major function. The first chance you get, attend one. They are *life changing events*! People make *life decisions* after gathering the facts presented and emotionally experiencing the event.

My husband, Richard, and I started our Nutrition For Life Business on August 22, 1994. Shortly afterwards, we met Dayle Maloney in Edmonton at a function where he was speaking.

Dayle came from the heart. He was such a comedian about this *serious* business. After meeting Dayle, Richard and I looked each other in the eye and said, "We can do this business!"

Dayle is very down-to-earth, a sort of "if-I-can-do-it, you-can-do-it" guy. In any business, if you don't believe you can do it, you'll quit. No matter what you do in life, there will be days you ask, "Why am I doing this?" If your belief level is not strong enough, you won't have a good answer for yourself. That's when you're in trouble.

As Dayle has said to us a number of times, "I'm sure I mentally quit this business 300 times the first year." It's comforting for us to know it's not a weakness for that to happen. We believe in the opportunity we've got here so we just keep doing it.

Dayle was in Canada for another large opportunity meeting. He told my twelve year old daughter, Nadia, "You look like a good Vanna White. We'll have you roll the drum for prizes at the end."

This was a *big event* for all of us. Dayle was putting everyone at ease. Nadia thought, "This is *so cool!*" She went up front, spun the drawing container and called the names out. Several years later, after all the events and people he's met, Dayle still asks about my daughter "Vanna." Nadia remembers him fondly as "Dayle, that Santa Claus guy who calls me Vanna."

What drew us to this business? Richard had money — but no time to enjoy it. I had no health as a result of multiple sclerosis. I have a quality of health today that I had given up on a long time ago.

The integrity of David, Jana and Dayle is incredible. They all came to visit our city and did a rally which gave us the opportunity to speak with them all one-on-one. That made the difference. They have put a great deal of trust in us. We could *never* leave them or let them down. We will always be there for them just like they will always be there for us."

Joanne and Richard Sokoloski and family

Success Secret ...

"You can work miracles by having faith in others. To get the best out of people, choose to think and believe the best about them."

Nutrition For Life Distributor Spotlight ...

Lloyd and Susan McCullough
1-Star Platinum Executives

"I've been in network marketing since 1976. On my next birthday, I will be 77 years old and plan on being with Nutrition For Life until they carry me out. Because I use Nutrition For Life products today, I can hike 15 miles — quicker than most anyone even half my age.

Good friends who are leaders in other companies have offered me great deals to join them. I would never go. I wouldn't even think of following anyone else. Two leaders offered me more money than I have made with this company. I know Nutrition For Life is headed in the right direction and will be around forever. I want to build my business once and then enjoy. I have about 700 people in my downline who think the same way."

— Lloyd McCullough
1-Star Platinum Executive, Oklahoma

Chapter 5

Can't Is A
Four Letter Word

PART 1

Be Thankful For No's

Congregation members gathered in our warmly lit church foyer as seating was starting in the sanctuary. Praise choruses echoed perfectly from floor-to-ceiling, comforting ears and securely blanketing souls. Children from Sunday school were quietly hustled up the blue carpeted isles between rows of chairs by their loving parents. When the church pianist finished, Pastor Dale Johnson jovially greeted the crowd.

As the service continued, Pastor Johnson announced a very special guest, the spokesperson from Habitat For Humanity. Recently, a Habitat For Humanity home was being constructed in northern Wisconsin with a fair market value of $80,000. The actual cost of the home — considering for each project, a large portion of labor and materials are donated — was about $35,000. The chosen new homeowner repays the actual building costs. The $45,000 or so in equity — between fair market value and building costs — is a financial miracle to a family who is living in substandard conditions but looking for a better standard of living.

Based on government housing figures, it was determined by Habitat for Humanity this part of Wisconsin was short on affordable housing. As town residents, we didn't need Washington, D.C. to tell us times were tough for a number of families in our community.

Being homeless just over a decade ago, Jeannine and I were particularly interested in her message. It rang clear and true in our hearts: too much month left at the end of the money — struggling to pay the rent and keep food on the table.

Living short on money takes a great toll on a person's heart, mind and body. You wake up in the morning to a heart flooded with fear as you wonder if this could be the last day this roof covers your head. By tonight, the locks could be changed and your possessions held for ransom or worse yet, scattered on the front lawn for you to gather, as your neighbors watch.

Imagine this morning you woke up in the comfort of your bed, but by this evening the privacy of your bedroom was in pieces on the lawn. Stripped of your dignity and security, as *strong* as you try to be, your heart breaks. Tears of anger and humiliation swell in your eyes and stream down your cheeks as you try to salvage as many of your belongings as you can carry in your arms. You have no where to turn, no where to call home, no where to feel welcome, stable or secure. It hurts.

After presenting her organization's history to the congregation, what she shared with us next brought us to our knees.

Based on the need in Wisconsin, I thought the competition would be great for the opportunity to experience the safety and security of affordable housing. We wondered, "What are the requirements to be the person or family who purchases the home for 50% or below fair market value?"

There are only 3 standards a family —single mom, single dad, or married couple — have to meet to qualify for a shot at an affordable home. Number one, they have to have a job. They have to work. Number two, they can't be on welfare. Number three, they have to agree over a *long* period of time to pay back the building costs of $35,000 at ZERO interest. Over 20-30 years that would be a house payment of about *$200 a month*! Reasonable qualifications — take action and make the call, have a job, go to work, get off welfare, and pay back a small home loan at no interest.

Normally, Habitat For Humanity has about 100 people answering the advertisements who are interested in applying for the house. How many people in the community where the home was built applied after they learned they needed a job, needed to pay back the loan, and needed to stay off welfare? *Four.*

If Habitat For Humanity can't bring 100 people to the table to *practically give away* a house, how badly should we feel when people can't see the opportunity Nutrition For Life has to offer?

You're going to get some "no's." We *all* get "no's." Think about it ... sometimes we're glad to get some "no's" and really people aren't saying "no" to you — they are saying no to themselves and maybe their future.

Would you want, as members of your business organization, the 96 people who did not apply for the near give-away home? They weren't willing to hustle to do what it took in return for an almost instant $45,000! We don't really need those people in the business. They aren't going to do anything for you or themselves. It's sad but true ... realize it is a blessing you hear some "no's." We all get them. Even Habitat for Humanity who's practically *giving away* a beautiful new home puts up with some "no's." Plus remember when you do get a "no," you are really just one "no" closer to the next "yes." So never be discouraged when you get a "no." Just say, "Next!"

Success Secret ...

"No person is totally worthless.
He or she can always serve as a
bad example."

PART 2

When Will You Ever Stop Talking About Money?

You're going to have folks tell you, "Oh, you're so materialistic — all you do is talk about making money." I hear that all day long.

Let me tell you something. You want to know when I was *materialistic*? WHEN I WAS BROKE! Back then, my mind was on money 24 hours a day.

The other night I watched an infomercial for Feed The Children. My heart throbbed from the sadness — I could hardly watch as they interviewed a little girl in Virginia, USA, who was visibly malnourished. Her torn, dirty clothing hung limp covering the contours of bones prodding through her skin. In the background was a bug infested mobile home with no plumbing and missing part of the roof.

During her interview, all she talked about was *food*. This 9-year-old girl lived every minute of her life with the terror of knowing she and her family were one meal from starvation. Shaking from the pain of not eating, she said into the camera, "I know if we don't get enough food we're probably going to die."

Look into the eyes of this child and explain to her that the money to buy the food she needs is not important.

If you don't want it for yourself, then think of all the pain you could remove from the hearts of children and adults. Think of how many little boys and girls you could feed with your money and success. If you can't find it in your heart to succeed for yourself, *please* succeed for them.

Success Secret ...

"The truest measure of a person is what he or she gives."

PART 3

What You See
Is What You Get

You will *always* find what you are looking for! If you want to see the *good* in a person or situation, you will *find* the good. The good *is always there*.

Try this. In a moment, when I ask you to, put this book down and look at your surroundings for as many red objects as possible. Look for red objects and count them. Do this for about 30 seconds and then come back to this page. Okay, start looking for RED items now. Okay, thirty seconds are over.

Now, I have a *very important* question to ask you. Please read it carefully and answer it *without* looking up from this page.

How many *GREEN* items did you see?

Success Secret ...

"If you are only seeing what you *don't* want, begin looking for what you *do* want."

PART 4

How A Rural Amish Farmer Became A Nutrition For Life Legend

The one success ingredient in life that has *never changed* is the dream. You absolutely have to have that dream. Thomas Jefferson once said, "I like the dreams of the future better than the history of the past."

Your dream has to be bigger than your excuses or your circumstances. Being broke is just a circumstance. Too busy? A circumstance. You have to always have the dream.

Lester Detweiler, an Amish farmer from Wisconsin, came to a Nutrition For Life meeting in December, 1985. It was a bone chilling cold night in Madison, Wisconsin, where the rain had dangerously turned to sleet and snow. The man who brought Lester was Greg Nettles who now lives in Maryland. After the meeting, Lester Detweiler wanted to enroll in Nutrition For Life. Back in 1985, it was a $12 enrollment.

I said, "Greg, don't you dare enroll him. If you do, you're stealing his $12." I stood firmly as I reasoned with Greg that Amish people have no car, no electricity, no telephone. "He doesn't have a chance. Please, Greg, don't accept his money." I pleaded.

"This man is different. He really wants to try it," Greg argued.

I said adamantly, "Greg, don't take it."

Greg Nettle took Lester's $12.

See, I didn't realize that Lester and Fanny Detweiler had a dream. They had owned three farms in Iowa. They sold those farms on land contracts. Then they used the down payment and bought four farms in Wisconsin — one for each of their three sons, keeping the home place for themselves.

In the mid-1980's, land prices throughout the Midwest tumbled. The Iowa contract buyers couldn't make their payments to Lester. He couldn't make his payments to the bank. His sizable net worth was gone.

When Lester came to the meeting in Madison, he was struggling, searching for some way to hang on to the home place. He made up his mind he would do whatever it took to keep the farm. I didn't realize that. I didn't know he had this dream.

The rest of the story is history. Here was a man that didn't own a car or drive one because of his religious beliefs. He had to hire a driver at 50 cents a mile to haul him around. He had a phone with a big bell on it out in the harness shop — no phone was allowed in the house. When you called Lester, it was best you let that phone ring about 10 minutes. He may have been a long ways out in the field, but he'd come running. "Detweiler, here," he'd gasp. Even today, they have no phone or electricity in the house, but back then this Amish man and his wife had a dream.

In 1994, Lester and Fanny Detweiler were the number three distributor in Nutrition For Life. In April 1994, from their farmhouse they sold 1,667 bottles of Requin 3 Shark Cartilage in one month.

In 1994, Lester and Fanny earned a free car through Nutrition For Life but their religious beliefs would not allow them to have one. Nutrition For Life President David Bertrand and Executive Vice-President Jana Mitcham said, "Lester and Fanny, you go out and find the buggy and team of horses of your choice and we'll make the payments."

Today, the Detweiler's drive a beautiful buggy that is pulled by a pair of Austrian Haplander horses. The rural Amish farmer and his family aren't struggling anymore. They are actually in retirement now.

Friend, if you have a dream, there is nothing that can stop you from taking this business right to the top. The dream is always going to keep you going.

Success Secret ...

"It is worse to dream poorly than not at all. Big dreams produce big results. Dream for the impossible! There is no competition at that level."

PART 5

We've Never Been This Far In Debt — How Do We Get Out?

Kurt Venekamp And Tim Goodwin,
4-Star Platinum Executives, Colorado
Saved From Financial Disaster

We owned two franchised restaurants in tourist areas of South Dakota, and it was tough going. Through hindsight, Tim and I learned franchises are over-rated and over-priced. In July, 1995, we were over $500,000 in debt with no idea how to get out. We owed everybody. We could only get our suppliers to deliver if we paid *cash*.

The weekend of July 10th, I was at the restaurant cooking and waiting on the counter because we couldn't find enough employees to work. Tim was gone that day. An old high school acquaintance of ours, Jack Lundie, asked me to take a look at an opportunity. Jack had been involved in different businesses over the years and had just joined Nutrition For Life. He thought this was the answer and wanted me to look at it. I knew I wasn't interested, but I looked anyway.

Jack must not have known how tough things were because if he did, he might not have even have showed us this opportunity. Tim and I had a dream to get out of debt. I signed us up that day, even though Tim was gone. When he returned to the restaurant I announced: "Tim, I think I've found the light at the end of the tunnel."

What was Tim's response? "Well, Kurt, we've spent money more foolishly than this." We didn't have the time to chase another business, we also didn't have any choice but to try. We were within a year of being forced out of business by our creditors and a 3rd partner.

Our fourth check from our Nutrition For Life business was $20,000. We realized there was serious money to be made in this program. In the beginning, we understood how the money would help people, but it took several months before we understood how the products, the training and personal growth were going to improve people's lives.

Because of Nutrition For Life, we were able to reduce our debt to a level that allowed us to sell our restaurants. Today, Nutrition For Life is making the payments for both our family's cars. We've had enough time and money to afford to travel. I was able to take 6 weeks off when my wife, Teresa, had a baby. I have lost weight, and friends of ours have walked away from life-threatening diseases. The residual income from our Nutrition For Life business allowed Tim to take the summer of 1996 off to travel, camp and go to the lake with his wife and daughter.

The opportunity to be trained and befriended by great leaders like Dayle Maloney, Kevin Trudeau, David Bertrand, and Jana Mitcham guarantees success when you can access mentorship from people who have gone before you and succeeded. It has changed our lives for the better in many ways over last 2 ½ years.

We have never met a guy with a bigger heart than Dayle Maloney. He has quietly helped people in our organization grow their businesses, and we didn't even know he was doing it. We're not even in his downline, and he sees no financial return from our organization but is always willing to help.

To see someone with *his* health and financial challenges accomplish what he has, it takes away anyone's excuses. If he ever decided to walk away from all of this, and we don't think he would, there would be a large void in Nutrition For Life. Dayle offers a different perspective on the business than anyone else can.

Dayle is the epitome of self-sacrifice. He is one of the most giving people we have ever met in this entire company — and that says a great deal because there are numerous very giving people in this organization. We've been involved in other network marketing companies — some of the big name companies — where the attitude is, "Well, if it helps me, if it benefits me, then I will take the time to do it."

Nutrition For Life has changed every part of our lives for the better. It has even enhanced the relationship Tim and I have with our families. Through this business we have both grown to where we have the guts to persevere and face challenges in other areas of our lives — where we wouldn't have four years ago. Tim and I realize we will be with Nutrition For Life forever.

Success Secret ...

"Never be so broke you cannot afford to pay attention!"

PART 6

How To Turn Defeat Into Dignity

As a teenager, I clung to the dream of graduating from high school at the top of my senior class. During my school years I set my trap lines in the cold, wet marshes and picked weeds from the dirt of local strawberry patches to earn enough money so my younger brother and I could keep going. I worked hard in high school all four years so at graduation I could be *the one* who addressed the senior class of 1953 as valedictorian — so I could "be somebody."

Senior graduation approached and I sat on "pins and needles" awaiting who would be named the valedictorian. Decision day came, and it was quietly announced that because no one had exceeded my grade point average, I was selected *momentarily* as the valedictorian. Yes, I said *momentarily*.

My year to shine and only during that year, for some unspoken reason, school officials decided *not* to have the valedictorian speak. The principal wouldn't talk to me about it. No one would listen or tell me why ... but in every inch of my body, I knew why.

What those people didn't know was I made a promise with myself: "I may be from the 'wrong-side-of-the-tracks,' but I'm not going to let the 'wrong-side-of-the-tracks' grow up in me!"

When my years of dreaming and working to give the

valedictorian speech were stripped away from me, do you think I didn't hurt? All the years of being teased, overcoming barriers built by people who *wanted* me to fail, it all hurt so bad my heart locked up — I couldn't breathe between my tears of anger and disgust. There wasn't a hole to crawl into that was deep enough. I was publicly stripped of any remaining dignity.

But even then, *my dream* was *bigger* than my hurt. In 1992, my niece, Tara, and in 1996, my nephew, Dana, gave the valedictorian speeches to their senior classes. It was redemption for what happened to me in 1953. I was so proud of both of them.

A few months later when I had polio, I had a lot of hurts again. The mind-crazing physical pain, the gut-wrenching fear of never walking again, the heart-crippling sadness of helplessly watching small children be paralyzed for life or even die.

How did I survive? A more relevant question is: "Why did I *choose* to survive?" I fought so hard to survive because I dreamed *someday* someone would ask me that very question. I had a dream someday you and many other people would embrace me and love me for *exactly* who *I am*. I had *dreams* that kept me *going* even when the journey to get there felt like it lasted <u>forever</u>. Friend, you and I, we've got to *have that dream*.

Success Secret …

"Without a dream …
you are simply without."

PART 7

The Greatest Danger in Network Marketing

I was mesmerized by the flashes of metal on the boy's shoulder walking past me. I stopped in my tracks and turned my whole body to follow his every move.

"Who is that?' I asked one of the local merchants who was watching me.

"That's Bobby," he said with a smile, "and those medals are for him bein' an Eagle Scout." The merchant was laughing as he turned to go back in and tend shop. My jaw hung to the sidewalk. With one glance I instantly wanted to be an Eagle Scout.

Shortly past my 12th birthday, I joined the Boy Scouts with the dream of moving up the ranks to Eagle Scout. I was ready to serve and obey — Scout's honor. The troop I joined had been together about 5 years. All the fathers participated in the activities — except mine. The town pretty much agreed the best place for Kenny Maloney was a bar stool. At least, you knew where to find him.

Twelve scouts were gathered around a table full of grasses, weeds and leaves to identify and name our green and brown subjects. We worked as a team because our troop could afford only one plant identification book, but we fought like the dickens to be the person who was important enough to call out the name of the plant.

"Maple leaf! That's a *maple leaf*, stupid!" the little brown haired, steely-eyed boy yelled across the table. I smeared glue on the back of the leaf, handing it to another boy to apply it to the cardboard.

"I hear Maloney thinks he's going to be an Eagle Scout!" a friend yelled to the other Scouts in the room. They all laughed.

My heart sank. Why did people laugh at me — when they didn't even know me? Where was our troop leader? Couldn't he tell them to stop? My eyes started searching but he was nowhere to be found.

Then the group chimed in, "Maloney's full of baloney. Maloney's full of baloney..."

That day I let another 12 year old Boy Scout *steal my dream* to be an Eagle Scout. Since that experience, I am tough on the dream stealers.

I've been able to *accomplish a great deal* and *help a lot of people* through network marketing. But the dream stealers in my home town of Eau Claire, still call me Captain Pyramid, King Vitamin, Commander Cookie, Sergeant Sudsy. They still try to tell me, "Oh, those things just don't work." Figure that one, will you? I have hundreds of stories to shoot holes in their "those things don't work" theories. I've shared only a small percentage of those stories in this book. I'd need to produce an encyclopedia if I were to give them all to you at once.

To succeed in network marketing or in life you have to avoid the dream stealers. Influence from a dream stealer is the number one cause of why people don't achieve their dreams. I despise dream stealers.

I've had 2 or 3 dream stealers who were so bad you almost wished birth control was retroactive — they can be that bad.

Do you know my definition of a dream stealer who thinks he or she is an expert? 'Ex' is a *has-been* and 'spert' is a *drip under pressure*. You and I, we've got no time for dream stealers. You'll never see a statue erected to a dream stealer. Most of them haven't had an original thought since soon after conception.

Male dream stealers in this area take their wives out one night a month. Do you know where they go — to K-Mart to chase the blue light specials. When a dream stealer remodels his home, he changes the shower curtain.

You know who the toughest dream stealers are? Husbands and wives who don't support each other. PLEASE, PLEASE SUPPORT EACH OTHER. You don't need someone in your *own home* trying to steal your dream.

Women who are out there building this business in the evening — you might be building your business alone or with your husband — and some people will say, "You're out there with *that thing* until *midnight*? You *ought* to be home with your children."

Take a look at the dream stealer who is criticizing

you. Most of them have a job from 9 to 5. Their kids are in daycare from 7 a.m. to 7 p.m. and they've got the guts to criticize *you* for being out building your business — trying to make a better life for your family? You are building a legacy that can be passed on for generations to come.

April 15, 1998, CNN aired a show on the price society is paying for putting children in daycare. Parents were visibly torn apart by having to leave their children for 10 to 12 hours, 5 days a week. The question was posed, "Do the children really know they are being left and does it affect them?" One man replied, "When my daughter is given the choice between going to daycare and spending time with her mother, mother wins *every time*." If you can't find it inside yourself to build this business for yourself, build it for your children. They love you a bunch and would do anything — including helping with the business —to spend more time with you.

The same week "Dateline" aired a show on the cost of daycare. They found a woman who grossed $15,000 ended up spending *$18,600* to keep her job after daycare, auto expense, work clothes, meals out, job related expenses, and over $4,000 in taxes. That means for this woman to break-even she would have to be *earning at least $10 for a minimum of 40 hours a week* to cover the additional taxes and her current expenses. That's $20,800 a year. Could people in these shoes use some additional income and lower tax bills? Unless they do something different, where are they going to be in 3 to 5 years? Start the business today and say good-bye to the rat race tomorrow.

And ladies, I don't want you to worry about keeping your house clean for the next *two* years. <u>Let</u> <u>it</u> <u>go</u>. Go out and *build this business* for the next two years. Let it go for two years and after that you can hire Merry Maids. They will keep your house clean for the *rest of your life*. Focus on your dream of making more than enough money from home and don't worry about what home looks like for now — circumstances change and houses will always be there to be cleaned.

We've got Merry Maids at our house. Three weeks ago we got a note on the door from our cleaner. She wanted to get involved in the business. I sponsored her in the business and at last Tuesday night's meeting she had *five prospects* in the second row. She sees there are better things than being a Merry Maid for the rest of her life.

Success Secret ...

"Knowledge is worthless when you are too scared to use it. Stay away from people who steal your dreams."

PART 8

One Little Push
For Success

A few months ago, I watched a documentary on eagles. They build their nests high in the trees or up in the cliffs.

On a certain day, all of a sudden the mother eagle takes *every single eaglet* and *pushes* it out of the nest. PUSHES THE EAGLETS OUT OF THE NEST! Awww, it was *so sad* to watch. Those little birds are bouncing off rocks. "Boom" some hit the ground — dead on arrival ... but the strong survive.

Why did she do it? Those little eaglets will never know what an honor it is to be born an eagle until they open those wings.

We're the same way, friend, all of us. From time-to-time we need a push out of the nest, too.

One day I was taking my two Maltese dogs, Barney and Benny, for a walk in the park. There were three little boys on the swings doing nothing. Their mothers were over at the picnic table gossiping. One little guy looked my way and asked, "Can I have a push?" I'd guess him to be about 6 years old. I pushed him and got him swinging high.

What do you suppose the other two wanted? A push. Pretty soon, I've got all three kids swinging.

All they needed was a little push. Sometimes, that's *all* we need.

People are so concerned about their downline liking them. Sometimes people would rather be popular with the downline than do what it takes to help the downline succeed.

Most of you contact your people to round them up for a meeting or training. You call and ask, "Joe, are you and Mary coming over Saturday morning for the workshop?"

"No, no a friend wants to go golfing (BLAH, BLAH, BLAH)," Joe says as he backs out.

You say politely, "Oh, okay Joe. You and Mary should try to make the meeting next week?"

Baloney! They should be at that meeting. Get *tough* with them. You get tough with your people and *help them become successful*. They won't just like you, they will love you. Don't worry about them liking you. You're doing good things for them. You're teaching them how to become successful. We all have to get that push-out-of-the-nest once in a while — every one of us.

We all have the same 24-hours a day in our wallet or purse. It's what *you do* with that time that counts. Nobody has 30-hours a day; we all have the same amount of time.

Make it productive time. Make it <u>positive</u> time. If you find yourself being negative — stop! It used to be said the squeaky wheel gets the grease. Things have changed. In today's world, more often the squeaky wheel *gets replaced.*

You're going to have to push yourself out of your comfort zone. You're not going to see freedom working *only* 40 hours a week. If that's what you think, you still have an employee mentality, and there is no freedom or security in that mindset.

You have to make your time count. Nobody can do that but you. You're the one who has to make it happen.

Success Secret ...

> "In Nutrition For Life, you've got to become the toughest boss you've ever had. When you do, you'll become the wealthiest employee you've ever seen."

PART 9

What Is Success In Network Marketing?

Kevin Trudeau, 5-Star Platinum Executive, Illinois
The Future Is Not A Gift; It Is An Achievement

Success in network marketing is not what "MLM experts" sell generically on tapes to the industry. Success in network marketing is earning a $100,000 check every month whether you go to work or not, and the check has been coming in for five years or more. That is a residual income. There are only a handful of people in network marketing who have reached that level.

Some people claim, "Well, I'm a success in network marketing. I *had* a downline of 100,000 people in this company." Well, if the company is gone, your downline is gone and you're not getting paid — then you had a job. Network marketing is when you do the work once — and you get paid for the rest of your life.

How many people have actually had that experience? Dayle Maloney is one of the few. When you look at those people who have achieved that level of success, you can usually find some common denominators. Generally, they are dynamic, charismatic, and maybe they are good communicators. They are positive, tenacious, and have a good work ethic.

What is surprising is when you look at Dayle Maloney, you find a person that if you were to consider sponsoring him, you probably wouldn't even approach him. What Dayle has done for the industry is really hit the nail-on-the-head. Don't prejudge anyone! You don't know what is *inside* a person — that is what is going to make the difference in whether they are successful or not.

People who think network marketing is the *only* way to make money are misled. Network marketing is just *one* vehicle to make money — it is a people-oriented business and best for those who want to deal with others. In terms of long-term residual income there is *nothing* better.

In terms of making money, look at the Fortune 500 — I don't see any network marketing people on there except Rich DeVos and Jay VanAndel. They are not distributors; they are company owners.

When it comes to making money in the world, you can do it a lot of different ways. In terms of lifestyle, there *is* a difference. A person can create a lifestyle with freedom of time, life-changing relationships, power and control over their life and own an empowering business which provides you residual income. When it comes to the lifestyle network marketing provides people, it stands head and shoulders above the rest.

When I picture Nutrition For Life's President David Bertrand, I think of the word "stewardship." Biblically, it talks about being a good steward of possessions because they are not yours — they are God's.

The dictionary defines a good steward as someone who takes care of things. If you were the steward for my estate, you would *take care* of my estate. You'd make sure that nobody was going to take it, steal it, or mess around with it. With a good steward in charge, if I could check on my estate, it would be in better condition that when I left.

David Bertrand is the perfect example of a good steward — which is exactly what is needed in a network marketing company from a corporate perspective. A good steward, as a distributor, wouldn't build because stewards protect what already exists. If I was protecting what I have, I wouldn't be building anything. There is a difference between a builder and a steward. David Bertrand is a perfect example of stewardship. As distributors, we put our trust in him to take careful and responsible care because if this company is not around, we don't have an income.

So while David is protecting what already exists, who is building? The leaders and their followers. Vince Lombardi said it best: "Leadership is kicking some people in the pants and patting some people on the back."

There are certain people who need a good, swift kick in the pants. There are others who need a firm pat on the back. A leader is not afraid to kick some people in the pants who should be patted on the back and pat people on the back that should be kicked in the pants. A leader is not afraid to make decisions that could result in a mistake. A leader leads and doesn't go for consensus but rather tells people where the group is going and the people follow. A leader is decisive — confident in his decision to move forward based on the bigger picture.

General Patton, when he was stuck in the mud in Sicily, decided his troops would not be stuck in the mud any more — they would move forward without any plan — it was Patton's decision to get up and move forward. All of his subordinates disagreed with his decision. Patton reminded them he was their commander and they were going to agree that moment or they would be relieved of their duties and positions. The troops moved forward, took heavy casualties and took over until Montgomery, the British commander, arrived.

Patton's troops had won the battle and achieved their objective but the commanders were still giving him criticism on the heavy casualties from the campaign. Patton reminded them, "Did you ever stop to consider how many casualties we would have had if we were still stuck in the mud back there?"

A leader may take some casualties, but he makes a decision for the greatest good, for the greatest number in order to move forward.

Kevin Trudeau, 5-Star Platinum Executive

Success Secret ...

"If you risk nothing, then you risk everything."

Can't Is A Four Letter Word

THE GREATEST SHOW
ON EARTH

FEATURING
DAYLE MALONEY AND
KEVIN TRUDEAU
STARRING IN
"CONSUMER EXPRESS"

December 3, 1985

THEATER LOCATION . . . . HILTON - JCT. HWY 35W & HWY 280 & HWY 36
N.E. MPLS. - INDUSTRIAL BLVD EXIT

SEATING AT 7:30 PM . . . SHOWTIME 8 PM TO 11 PM

TICKETS . . . . $5.00 EACH PERSON BEFORE 8 PM
AFTER 8 PM $ 4,782.37 EACH PERSON

CAST OF CHARACTERS . . .

DAYLE MALONEY . . . THE TOP # 1 DISTRIBUTOR FOR CONSUMER EXPRESS
KEVIN TRUDEAU . . . "BOY WONDER" FINANCIALLY INDEPENDANT BY AGE
CHUCK SANDERS . . . JANITOR

SUPPLIES NEEDED . . . . ONE LARGE BAG. WE WILL SUPPLY YOU WITH SO
MUCH INFORMATION & INSPIRATION & MOTIVATION,
YOUR BRAIN WILL NOT HOLD IT ALL.

P.S. TO SAVE TIME AT THE TICKET OFFICE HAVE CHECKS ALREADY MADE
PAYABLE TO CHUCK SANDERS.

*Author's Note: Dayle Maloney and Kevin Trudeau
have been good personal and business friends since their first
meeting on December 3, 1985.*

PART 10

Can One Person Really Make A Difference?

Come to my office in Eau Claire, and go through my desk drawers full of testimonials, I'll guarantee you won't have a dry eye after 15 minutes. The stories of what people in Nutrition For Life have done to touch the lives of people all across the globe are incredible. I feel many of us have made a difference.

I want to share a story about one person who made a difference. Terry Fox, a young college student in British Columbia, came down with cancer in 1977. He said, "I'm going to make a difference. I want to show Canadians and the world the stuff I'm made of. I will not let anybody call me a quitter."

Terry Fox is the man who attempted in 1980 to run across Canada from St. John's, Newfoundland, all the way to Stanley Park in Vancouver, B.C. Friend, Terry had lost a leg to cancer. He ran on one artificial leg and a crutch.

Do you think he started running across Canada the first day he made the decision? Terry ran and practiced for 18 months. He ran over 3,000 practice miles before he started his cross-country run. We also have to get in shape in our business, practice makes perfect. That's why when you start, you will talk to more people and sponsor fewer, but later you will talk to fewer people and sponsor more.

In our business the race doesn't start overnight either. You've got to practice. You get better every day with more practice — calling prospects and showing the plan.

He left St. John's, Newfoundland, on April 12, 1980 heading for Vancouver. Terry ran a-marathon-a-day for *146 straight days* with one artificial leg and a crutch. His short term goal was to raise $1,000,000.00 for cancer research. His long-term goal was to raise $1.00 from every Canadian, which was $24,000,000.00.

Terry Fox became one of my heroes. I've done some speaking for the Terry Fox Foundation. I've talked to his mother and brother. It's incredible what's happened because of Terry Fox.

Can you imagine this courageous young man running with an artificial leg and a crutch — trying to raise money for cancer? Believe it or not, the press was *negative* towards Terry Fox ... and people think the press has been negative to the network marketing industry. Let me print a few quotes, what the press said as Terry Fox, the man with a dream, was running across Canada.

The *Peterborough Examiner* called it, "A folly."

Broadcaster Gordon Sinclair called Terry, "... a three legged horse that ought to be stopped."

The *Toronto Globe & Mail* wrote, "... running

because he held a grudge against a doctor," and "It was the cancer society that made it a success. He was only doing the running."

Yah sure, a-marathon-a-day for 146 days with a cancer-stricken body, one artificial leg and a crutch, and Terry was *only* doing the running. See, we all face adversity.

Terry Fox was in Thunder Bay, Ontario when he had to quit on September 1, 1980, because the cancer had spread to both lungs. Terry went home. He passed away on June 28, 1981, at 4:30 a.m. (his favorite time of the day).

Today, Terry Fox is probably the *number one* hero in all of Canada. There are buildings, highways and mountains named in his honor.

Can one man make a difference? *Absolutely!* Terry Fox left a legacy. I want to see *you* leave a legacy with Nutrition For Life. That's what *I'm* going to do. My dream is to leave a legacy.

Terry Fox didn't raise $24,000,000.00. He didn't raise $1,000,000.00.

The Terry Fox Run now is held the third Sunday of every September around the world and they are raising in the neighborhood of *$50,000,000.00* for the Cancer Society every year. **One person can make a difference.**

When he died, here's what the *Toronto Globe & Mail* — the same paper that criticized him — said: "Terry Fox's race is over. In fact, he never finished the course. None of us do. What is important is the running. What is important is to set goals. What is important is not to quit, not ever. What is important is to run well and honestly with as much human grace as possible, not forgetting to take joy in the running."

Before Terry passed away, with the final moments of life running through his body, he said, " I guess one of the most important things I've learned is that nothing is ever completely bad, even cancer. It has made me a better person. It has given me the courage and a sense of purpose I never had before. You don't have to do like I did — wait until you lose a leg or get some awful disease — before you take the time to find out what kind of stuff you are really made of. You can start now — anybody can. What kind of stuff are you made of?"

What kind of stuff are you made of?

I tell you his story because it proves to you one person absolutely can make a difference. And that's what I want to see you do, each and every one of you.

Success Secret ...

> "You have a mission to go out there and absolutely make a difference."

PART 11

What You Do Speaks So Loudly I Can't Hear Your Words

John Morgan,
1-Star Platinum Executive, Nova Scotia, Canada
Talking The Talk And Walking The Walk

Dayle Maloney is a guy who didn't know me from Adam. The folks here in the Eastern Maritime Provinces of Canada were having some problems getting Dayle's product training information through customs in a timely manner, and I let Dayle's office know about it.

The next thing I knew, UPS pulled up in my yard and unloaded *$7,000* worth of training tools into my house.

Shocked, I called Dayle to find out what was going on. He told me, "Sell it and send me the money when you collect it."

What the heck am I going to do? Nobody does this in business today. <u>He</u> <u>doesn't</u> <u>even</u> <u>know</u> <u>me</u>. I could have wheeled all the stuff away and sold it for half price, kept the money and said, "Too bad." C'mon think about it. What would you have done?

I am so many levels down from Dayle's pay-lines that he's not even collecting money on me or my downline. Would most people help others like that?

The guy *loves the business*. He *IS* the business. He *IS* Mr. Multi-Level Marketing.   Dayle's got respect from everyone I know of in multi-level marketing — even in different companies.   Dayle Maloney's generosity is unbelievable.

He flew to Nova Scotia on his own dime to do a meeting for us. I know he makes good money, and you might rationalize he could afford to do it. But there are a lot of people out there making more money than Dayle Maloney — who wouldn't spend 5 cents on you because money is their life. With Dayle Maloney *the people* are his life.

Now, *we invited Dayle* out for dinner with our downline leaders. We couldn't get seating at the first restaurant. The only restaurant that could seat the 15 of us was this real ritzy place.

Because of our economy, many residents of Nova Scotia are financially challenged. My newly sponsored networkers were looking at the menu in a panic like, "Oh, no! This is the *whole weekend's budget* going for one meal." It was hard for me to watch them order.

Every meal was $16.95 or more. The couples were

really squirming because that's at least a $50 dinner with the beverages and a tip.

We were placing our orders. Dayle was in the center of the group and the waitress asked for his order. He said, "I'm just making up my mind, you go ahead."

We all placed our orders and the waitress came back to Dayle. He placed his order and said, "By the way, put this all on one check ... it's mine."

We gasped! With tip and tax that was about a $500 check. Our faces just hung open.

C'mon, this guy wasn't even making any money off of us. We're so far out of his pay-line it isn't even funny. He spent *his own money* to come here *just to inspire us* to achieve our dreams.

Dayle called me the other day and asked me to come to speak to a group in Eau Claire. Now Eau Claire's got nothing to do with my downline. What do you think I said? I said, "Sure, I'll be there tomorrow if you want."

Everyone in Nutrition for Life owes everything they have to Dayle Maloney. Dayle wasn't an overnight success. He's not a flamboyant man. Dayle's appeal is that he's a big-hearted guy. He's the father or grandfather you wish you had.

John Morgan and his lovely wife, Charlot
1-Star Platinum Executive, Nova Scotia, Canada

Success Secret ....

"The person who has much is not rich,
but the person who gives much is."

PART 12

Stability and Consistency

David Moreno, Stockbroker, Colorado
People May Doubt What You Say,
But They Will Believe What You Do

During the normal course of a day, I deal with large amounts of money. I see how money affects people and with Dayle, the focus is on how the money can help people. I've known him for several years. He's amassed a great amount of wealth of which he's given much away. I handled the church transaction where Dayle invested a sizable amount of money in stock and it turned into about $400,000. Dayle gave well over $400,000 to build a church.

As a 10-year veteran stockbroker, I usually hear, "I want all the money myself." But from Dayle I hear, "I want to turn it over to this cause or that cause." Dayle is a wonderful, wonderful human being.

David Bertrand, Jana Mitcham and Dayle Maloney have been together since nearly the beginning of the company. I think it is a great service to the distributors to make this story available. It is important to show how Dayle, David and Jana — all people of high integrity — have stuck together.

Dayle contributes greatly to the stability and integrity of this company. As some people come and go, Dayle's organization continues to grow with constancy.

David Moreno

Nutrition For Life is a publicly held company on NASDAQ (symbol: NFLI). For questions on Nutrition For Life stock or for shareholder information you may call David Moreno at 800-634-2770 or 303-764-6040. David is an Investment Consultant with Kirkpatrick Pettis which is a Mutual of Omaha Company. He is Dayle Maloney's personal stockbroker.

Success Secret...

"Protect your credibility. One of the greatest honors is the comment, 'If (he or she) says so, you can take it to the bank.'"

PART 13

Are You
Ready To Quit, Yet?

I admit I've had plenty of times when I was ready to quit. I took immediate action on my feelings. The difference is the *type* of action I decided to take. I made the choice to keep going. Somehow, you've got to keep going. Why?

If you have times when you're ready to quit, *you're half way home to success.* If you're at the point of chucking-it-all, it means you've made it over the hump, the hard work is over … it's going to get a lot easier from here.

I always say, "In the beginning you do a lot you don't get paid for. Then later, you get paid for a lot you don't do."

People ask me, "Who makes it in Nutrition For Life?"

My answer? One hundred percent of those who *choose* to make it, make it in Nutrition for Life. It's the people who <u>choose</u> to do it that make it happen. I've met thousands of people who *wouldn't* do this business, but I've never met anyone who *couldn't* do the business.

What stops some people? What keeps *them* from making it? **The "no's!"**

We all have "no's" and no-shows. If I had a dollar for every "no," every no-show, and every no-no-show I've had, I'd take you and your entire family — aunts, uncles, cousins ... the whole works — to Hawaii for a week. The no show is when I come to do a meeting at your home and the four couples that were coming have cancelled. That's a no-show. But if I come out to your house and *you* aren't even there, that's a no-no-show. I've had them where I walked up to the porch and the porch light goes out and I can here them inside going SHHHHH SHHHHH. That's a no-no-show.

"No's" are okay. We haven't got room for *everyone* to go full-time with Nutrition For Life. If *everyone* went full-time, when you dined at a restaurant, you'd have to *take your own order and cook your own food.* If you went to the hospital, you'd have to *operate on yourself.* Be thankful some folk still want to have a regular J-O-B — which means they Jump Out of Bed every morning.

Have you heard about my proposed no-show picnic? The 2,500 no-shows I've had over the last 10 years are going to be mailed a beautiful two-color invitation. It will read: "Come to my big picnic at Carson Park at 1:00 p.m., two weeks from Saturday. Free barbecue ribs, pork, beef, coleslaw, potato salad, baked beans. All-you-can-eat. All-you-can-drink. FREE."

About 12:30 p.m. that day, I will have caused the biggest traffic jam in the history of Eau Claire! When 1:00 p.m. comes, *I'll* be the *no-show.* There won't be any picnic. I'll get revenge for all of us for all those times in business where you showed up to a meeting and your prospect was nowhere to be found.

Success Secret ...

"When you invite ten people to a meeting and six don't show, what is most important are the four people in the chairs. At that moment, ignore the six no-shows."

PART 14

Thinking Outside the $40,000 A Year Box

Marilyn Reid,
1-Star Platinum Executive, Alberta, Canada
The Magic of Big Ideas

I am a registered nurse. My husband, Robert, is also a government employee. In 1994, the Canadian government was cutting back its workforce, and we were both frightened that our salaries could be lost overnight. We decided to be proactive and try to find another source of income.

I attended Dayle Maloney's *Secrets of MLM Seminar* and purchased his audio tape program. During the seminar, he did not talk *specifically* about Nutrition For Life but eluded to the fact that he had substantial income from another source outside his seminar business. He had built it to the point that regardless if he didn't do another thing, he would receive a large check every month. This caught my ear because it was what we were looking for — something we could build once and benefit for a lifetime.

When everyone was gone I asked Dayle, "C'mon, is what you're doing legal? And if it is legal, is it moral?" Dayle said he was having great success in his Nutrition For Life business. He gave me a little bit of information and told me I could join with him.

Two days later, Robert and I left for our anniversary get-away weekend. We drove 1½ hours to the hotel where Dayle's next meeting was being held to personally hand Dayle our Nutrition For Life application.

At that point in my career, I was open to looking at what nutrition could do for people. I was still very skeptical because of my medical training and 20-years of nursing. On July 1, 1994, I spoke directly to Jana Mitcham, our Executive Vice-President. I was very impressed with her knowledge of the products. As a result, I placed a product order.

I have felt life-changing results from the shark cartilage. When I was 4 years old, I fell out of a moving car. I had a neck injury which resulted in a lifetime of on-going headaches. I tried Nutrition For Life's shark cartilage and to my total amazement it worked!

Was it the shark cartilage that helped? I did take it easier that summer. Maybe it was an air pressure change. All I know is, when I stopped taking the shark cartilage, the headaches came back. I had been on all kinds of medication trying to control the onset of headaches. The only other pain relief I found was codeine. It was totally unbelievable to me that a *natural supplement* could do this for me.

I had one more disbelief to overcome. I certainly didn't think anyone could make money in network marketing. When I started my business, the only person I had ever met who had made money in network marketing was Dayle Maloney. I wasn't even exactly sure what network marketing was. What I did know was, I felt I could trust Dayle Maloney. I'm proud to say today I know many people, including myself, who make *good money* in network marketing.

Being around people who dream big and have big

goals can have a huge impact on your life. I work in a setting with budget cut backs and restructuring. At the hospital they want us to do more with less staff. The atmosphere can be full of negative, small thoughts. We discovered that Robert and I thought small ourselves. We were thinking inside the "$40,000-a-year-box." Before Nutrition For Life, our dreams were based on $40,000 a year. We've already achieved goals outside that box and we're still going!

**Marilyn and Robert Reid have three children:
Cathy, 12, Jennifer, 14, Bobby, 7.**

Success Secret ...

"A person with big dreams is more powerful than a person with all the facts."

PART 15

There Is More To Life Than The 40/40/40 Rut

People are getting tired of the 40/40/40 rut. We work 40 hours a week for 40 years and they give us a $40 watch when we retire — and now they are skimping on the watches. There is more to life than *the rut*. Hey, you need to keep the job for a while! I'm not going to ever tell you to quit the job prematurely. But give Nutrition For Life *every hour* that *you can*.

I used to work two full-time jobs. I worked Nutrition For Life from 9 a.m. to 5 p.m. From 5 p.m. to midnight I worked the second shift of — Nutrition For Life. You know why? Because I *love* it!

I guarantee you this: You will like this business better than your regular JOB. There is no comparison. This is fun. People ask, "Why do you go 14 to 16 hours a day, every day, Dayle, when you don't have to?" Because IT'S FUN!

Where else can you impact the lives of other people in a positive way and give them better health *and* better wealth? Where else do you have the freedom to stretch your wings and use your gifts and talents? There is no other place, friend. You get involved with Nutrition For Life and you lose track of your bonus checks. That check will show up correct and on time in your mailbox. You'll give thanks and keep on moving. You will find yourself to be driven to go out and help other people.

There are four things you need to succeed in this business:

Number one: You have to have trust. You have to believe in network marketing. You have to believe in Nutrition For Life. You have to believe in your upline.

Number two: You have to be a giver. You can't *out give* in this business. The more you *give* your *people*, the more *you'll* always *get back*. There are times I've given to the point most people couldn't comprehend, but I've always received back <u>more</u> than I've given. Maybe not from the person who I gave to, but *somehow* it always comes back. Have trust. Be a giver.

Number three: Expect good things. When you have *trust* and you're a *giver,* good things will come your way.

Number four: *You* have to be *trustworthy* yourself. Your <u>word</u> must *be your bond*.

Success Secret ...

"Have trust. Be a giver.
Expect good. Be trustworthy."

PART 16

Leaders Help Others Reach Their Goals

Mark Hull, Northern Wisconsin Director of The Fellowship of Christian Athletes, Wisconsin

Dayle and Jeannine Maloney's financial support and provision of a free office really helped the Fellowship of Christian Athletes in northwestern Wisconsin during a difficult financial time for us.

Dayle promised, "My hat's in the ring." I discovered that means, "I am going to make sure you succeed." That's exactly what he has done. He is a great marketer and has given us solid direction: "We need to do a banquet. Let's go out and book a speaker." He hired Mike Singletary, Hall of Fame Linebacker from the Chicago Bears, as the speaker.

Dayle underwrote our whole first year's banquet. This gave us a new level of exposure which launched us in a whole new way. Dayle & Jeannine are encouraging people who really believe what we do is a wonderful investment of their funds. They look at the eternal returns on those funds for generations to come.

Success Secret...

"It may be that those who do the most, dream the most."

Is Nutrition For Life The Right Company For You?

Chris McGarahan,
4-Star Platinum Executive, California
Why People Join Nutrition For Life

Why do people join Nutrition For Life? There are 5 reasons:

1) **The Company.** Nutrition For Life has been in business almost 14 years which proves it is a solid company. Wake up any morning, open your newspaper to the NASDAQ stock exchange pages and look for the symbol NFLI — which is Nutrition For Life's symbol — we are a publicly traded company. That also adds an immense amount of credibility.

My first impression of our founders, David Bertrand and Jana Mitcham, was they were very solid. I knew they had been with the company since day one. Being a successful businessman, I knew what it took for them to build a strong network marketing company. Many companies have failed because of lack of integrity within the leadership — obviously, these people have integrity and all the assets it takes to stay in the game.

2) **The Products.** The company you join must offer consumable products. If your organization and their customers can't *use* the product monthly, they won't *purchase* it monthly. Only when product volume is moved monthly will you have residual income. This company has life-changing, consumable products that people will buy and use every month.

3) **The Compensation Plan.** The greatest compensation plan in the world has a method for the part-time network marketer to earn money as well as full-time networkers. Nutrition For Life has both — it is fair to everybody. There are no high inventory or purchasing requirements like a number of other companies demand.

4) **The Training and Support.** Nutrition For Life has good training and strong support for new distributors when they join so they can immediately build their businesses, earn income and enjoy success.

5) **The Timing.** If everybody in America has already heard about the opportunity, it is going to be hard to sponsor more people. The business opportunity

cannot be overexposed. There are millions of prospects for Nutrition For Life distributors.

A part of your personal success in Nutrition For Life is to have an interest in the products offered. There is no point in joining a network marketing company unless you and other people can use and consume the products monthly. Just to see if you qualify to come into the business opportunity, please answer the follow:

"Do you or anyone you know brush their teeth?"

"Do you or anyone you know use laundry detergent and household cleaners?"

"Who do you know who uses shampoo to wash their hair?"

"Who do you know who eats food ... yes, eats food?"

Hmmm, it seems you have qualified to join this business opportunity because we have products you are already using every month in your household. All you have to do is replace your existing vendor and purchase these products from your own business and in doing so you will be paid a commission.

We also have very high-end nutritional products you cannot find anywhere else which are very popular in today's marketplace. One of the fastest growing franchises right now is a company called GNC — General Nutritional Centers. You could invest a few hundred to a few thousand dollars in a Nutrition For Life business and receive a complete business building system with a potential for an incredible return of residual income or you could choose to spend tens of thousands of dollars to work a nutritional franchise.

Some network marketing companies sell just one non-consumable product and once the people in your organization and their customers have purchased that product, they don't need it again. Say a company sells a burglar alarm. Once people have purchased the burglar alarm — that's it — they won't need to buy it again.

Because they do not want to purchase a burglar alarm over and over again, it will not produce residual income for you. What you have just done is bought yourself a sales job.

The products in Nutrition For Life are highly consumable: food, shampoo, soap, nutritionals, just to name a few. Because Nutrition For Life offers over 380 products and 95% are consumable products people are already using, they order every month to replace what they use. This is what builds residual income.

Most of the dream stealers I have seen in my work with distributors are family members: spouses, brothers, sisters, cousins, mothers, fathers, even sons and daughters.

Dream stealers don't like their loved ones to change. It is so critical when you are offering the business opportunity to a married person that the spouse also sees it at the same time. I don't even set an appointment unless I am showing the plan to both people.

Why? If the husband likes it and he wants to sign up, or does sign up, there is a real high percentage when he arrives home his wife isn't going to like it because he can't explain it in detail that night to her. Therefore, you could potentially lose a good person by not showing the plan to both spouses at the same time. Until I show the plan to both spouses, I don't sign either of them up!

If you do sign one person up then what you have is someone who can't really do the business because they don't have the support of the people in their home. They will be ridiculed even if they try to build a business: "Oh, you've been out again and it didn't work, did it?" or "Oh, you're going to another one of those silly meetings."

Any business commitment works only if you have both spouses in the game. Do both people have to be actively building the business? No, it just means one is supporting and encouraging what the other is doing. My wife doesn't actively build our Nutrition For Life business, but she supports me while I am building the business. Whether it is the man or the woman building the business, there has to be support at home. While the business is being built, there are going to be time sacrifices — things you can't do with your family because you are building to give them a better life.

Another way to solidify the situation is to have the spouse attend a function and let them see the type of people who are involved. A large portion of network marketing is the social aspect — the relationships you build. When the person who is not building the business meets the type of people involved, maybe meets another wife or husband who is in the supporting role, they can then talk to the other person and become friends. They have a common ground. Relationship building is very important in overcoming dream stealers.

I think Dayle Maloney is a diamond out of the sky, a saint. Through the "grapevine" I discovered he has donated over $400,000 to build a church. He has helped people in his downline who were financially challenged. Dayle has been extremely generous to young people and people getting started in the business, and of this he says very little.

He has done so much — at times it seems almost too much — which is the key to his success. He gives so much that when it comes back to him it is ten-fold. Sometimes he doesn't receive it in return right away … but it does come back. It's hard to say when to give and when not to, so just give. It may not come back in the form you gave; it may come back in a completely different way.

When Edison invented the light bulb it wasn't a spectacular thing *then*, but it is today because it produces neon lights, fax machines, computers and more. Great people make people's lives better forever. Bill Gates would not be Billionaire Bill without electricity — because computers wouldn't work. Networking marketing a 100 years from now will take a completely different form. It may be done on some technology we haven't yet discovered, but it couldn't have been started without people like Dayle Maloney. The whole industry really has been started by just a handful of people. What Dayle Maloney has accomplished probably has in a very positive way changed and affected people's lives and the future of network marketing. In our industry, Dayle Maloney invented the light bulb.

There will continue to be books written about Dayle Maloney 30 to 40 years from now. Dayle Maloney will be remembered as a pioneer in network marketing. Whatever network marketing is going to be in the future, it will be credited to him. He has affected thousands of people's lives and some of those people will carry on his work. I believe Dayle Maloney will not see his *greatest* credits today — he is like Picasso or Van Gough – it was after the great artists were gone people gazed into a piece of art and realized what they held in their hands. Even though during his lifetime Dayle has received recognition, I believe his true glory may not be for 25 years or more. Let's hope he is still here with us.

Chris and Stacy McGarahan have three children:
Amanda, Christopher and Katie.
They started with Nutrition For Life in January, 1996.

Success Secret ...

"A successful person develops their ordinary qualities to more than an ordinary degree."

Chapter 6

Can They Fog A Mirror?

PART 1

It's Not Who *You* Know, It's Who *They* Know And Who *Their* People Know

When I first started in 1983, I held a 7:30 p.m. opportunity meeting for a brand new distributor in Missoula, Montana.

He was so excited I was coming out. "I've got them all lined up. This is a *big* event!" he announced as we talked about the size of the room. We covered every detail except the ambiance of the meeting facility.

When I pulled into the motel in Missoula, I couldn't

believe my eyes. I think we would have drawn more people on the street corner — at least they would have felt safer. If I hadn't promised to be the speaker, I'm not sure I would have stepped foot in that building. It was a terrible place — wall paper hanging off the walls, light bulbs burned out, a dirty, musty odor — the kind that quickly penetrates your clothes and stays with you through a couple washings. But to my distributor it was perfect, and soon all his friends and relatives would be joining us for the 7:30 p.m. meeting.

My watch read 7:15. "Maybe it's a few minutes fast," I said tapping the face of the watch as I tried to comfort my new distributor. It was near meeting time and nobody had showed up.

About 7:25 p.m. embarrassment overcame my distributor. "Hey, it happens to all of us. I've had hundreds of no-shows. It's okay," I persuaded — but it wasn't enough. He got mad and retreated to the corner where he quit.

I stuck around to see if anyone would show up. About 7:30 p.m. a young kid strolled down the hall. He was quite a sight to behold — long scraggly hair, torn clothing. He looked rough and needed a good scrubbing. He said, "I'm lookin' for the meetin'. "

I shook his hand and said, "C'mon in." He said his name was Kevin.

"Kevin, what do you do?"

"Not much." It seems Kevin cut grass two or three days a month for two local motels ... that's all he did.

"Kevin, sit in the front row. Those are the *money seats*. We have a lot more folks coming real soon." You guessed it ... nobody else showed up.

It was a long walk from the back of the room to where I needed to be at the front. Here was my distributor over in the corner — he wouldn't look at me, he was pouting, he was mad, he had quit. Here was Kevin in the front row all excited.

Speaking as if there were thousands of people in that audience, I came to the final close. I like to close by getting out the application and saying while nodding my head up and down, "Well, what do you think?"

Kevin was excited. He wanted in right now. The enrollment was $49 but Kevin had a problem, he said, "I've only got $18. I may not have any more money for two or three weeks."

I replied, " I believe in you, Kevin. I'm going to loan you $31, today." I wanted to get my distributor rejuvenated. We got this young kid his success kit and he left.

A few days later Kevin cut the grass at a motel south of Missoula. He showed the success kit to the manager, Bob, and said, "Look what I got suckered into."

Bob says, "Wait a minute Kevin, I'm trying to find one of these networking companies. Do you suppose you can get me involved with you?"

"I guess so," Kevin sighed. "Here's the junk the guy gave me. Plus you've got to fill something out. Here, Bob, you can have it all." It became a self-service enrollment, but here is the rest of the story ...

Bob went on to become the *number three* distributor

in a company with *over 275,000 distributors*.

If they're breathing — you get them in. They might be the one you're looking for or they'll lead you to the one you want. Most of my top people were sponsored by somebody else, I didn't get them. If they can fog a mirror, you've got to get them in and get them in right away!

Hold meetings to meet your enrollees' people. Give them support, and see if you can find a live one. Remember, it's not who *you* know that counts. It's who *they* know and who *those* people know and who *those* people know that counts.

Success Secret ...

"A small hinge opens a big door.
Every loser knows at least one winner."

PART 2

Where There Is A Will, There Is A Way

Ed Brandrick, 3-Star Platinum Executive, Canada
If It Is To Be — It Is Up To Me

I was a truck driver with a 6th grade education and home only 7 days out of a month. I didn't have a whole lot of time to dedicate to my Nutrition For Life business. I did sponsor a few people and held meetings with them when I was not driving truck. We all worked together to build the organization. In 1½ years, my Nutrition For Life income replaced what I made from my job so I retired from truck driving and went full-time network marketing.

When I started I didn't search out "heavy-hitters." I worked with anybody and everybody who had a dream. I gave everybody a chance at the opportunity and helped them as much as I could to build their businesses. I know today, my organization is built well past my 30th level. I'd guess it has a couple thousand people. I know for sure in my matrix, I have 750 executives.

What do I recommend people do to succeed?

First, you find the reason you are doing network marketing. What is your dream? What in your life haven't you achieved, yet?

Then, you make your prospect list, the list of everybody you know — not just certain people, but everybody you know. Yes! Offer this to your family; give them the opportunity. If they say "no," you can always go back to them later. When people say "no," what they are really saying is they want to wait and see what *you* do with it first.

I offered the opportunity to my family. I have sisters who today are not yet in the business. This is crazy! They have six years of university education, good paying jobs and can't see the vision. I have less than a grade school education with a farmer/truck driver background and I make four times as much money as they do.

How many people have I personally sponsored? About 30 people, and around 18 are actively building the business. I started my business in 1994. I had people quit who where on my first level back then. Today, the four people who are in those positions are now all driving free cars and making thousands of dollars each month.

When I speak at meetings, I ask, "How many people have been to network marketing school?"

People choose network marketing as a business, know nothing about it, and expect to be successful. You must invest time into understanding why people have not been successful in network marketing. It helped me to know why average people weren't successful with the different types of network marketing plans, and people would tell me, "I was in one of those before, and it didn't work."

I could say, "Look, let me show you why that other compensation plan couldn't have possibly worked, why it wasn't your fault and how you can succeed with our plan." The secret is to help people see what *we* have, compared to what they had before. The result? Their belief level rises, and they become more convinced in their hearts that they have something really good to offer people.

Ed Brandrick with his car which is paid for
by Nutrition For Life.

Success Secret...

"Great accomplishments are achieved not by strength but by perseverance."

PART 3

Escape From Corporate America

Mike and Pam Nadeau,
2-Star Platinum Executives, Wisconsin,
How To Replace Your White Collar Income

I was successful in Corporate America making over $100,000 a year. I had the "golden handcuffs" — a high-stress, pressure-loaded position in the finance and insurance field making just enough money that I couldn't walk away.

At age 42, I had a heart attack from the stress load and realized if I wanted to live to see 45, I would need to somehow replace the income from my high-pressure job. Approaching my mid-40's, I was worried and wondered, "How will I find a career with little or no stress where I can earn over $100,000 a year?"

The only thought that came to my mind was I didn't want anything to do with network marketing. I was not going to sell soap to my neighbors.

As a favor to a friend in 1989, I attended a network marketing opportunity meeting where I watched people walk across the stage and give testimonials on their financial success. They were making the kind of money I was looking for. Many of them did not have my kind of business experience or background. I stared in amazement and said, "If they can do it, I can do it." I asked what it took to join. They said to start right, I would need to invest $25,000. I wrote the check that night. The next morning I called the bank and took out a second mortgage on the house to cover the check.

My wife, Pam, and I worked ourselves to the top of the pay plan, but the company we were with went out of business. We joined another company — achieved the same — and it went out of business.

I met Dayle Maloney at a generic network marketing seminar he was giving. He asked me to attend a small meeting in Minneapolis. His idea of a small meeting and mine were totally different.

I said, "Dayle, I'll go, but I don't want anyone to know I'm attending."

He replied, "Mike, don't worry. You just sit in one of the back rows. I think you'll blend in just fine."

When I walked in the room, much to my surprise, there were 1,200 people attending Dayle's "small meeting."

I took a seat in the last row. Dayle was on stage and midway through his presentation he said, "We have many top industry leaders joining Nutrition For Life right now, and one of them is looking at us today: Mike Nadeau would you stand up...."

That's how it all started. I joined February 11, 1996 and signed up 19 executives in my first week and within 90 days was Platinum.

When I started down this path, I had no idea it would be my escape from corporate America — but it has been — and many others are joining me. Why? It's the lifestyle network marketing provides.

I enjoy a high monthly income from this business which has more than replaced my corporate America income but without the stress. Today, my business lifestyle includes plenty of time with my wife and family working towards common goals. My family and I traveled over 50,000 miles together to build this business last year — *not* because we had to — but because we wanted to. We love the fun and excitement of visiting many different cities and making friends across the country. We live most of our time together like we are on one big expense-paid vacation.

My 26 year old son, Chris, who is in Philadelphia, is also an NFL distributor. He attended the National Convention in 1997 and spent time with Dayle. Then they did a couple of events together out on the East Coast. Dayle is leaving a legacy with the second generation of my family.

Why is my family so important to me?

This story about little Johnny who came home and wanted his daddy to play with him will explain:

Johnny's father came home from work and was tired. The father sat on the couch and played with Johnny for a couple of minutes. Johnny's dad looked down on the table and saw a magazine with a picture of the world on the front cover. He tore the magazine cover off and ripped it into several pieces, handed the pieces to Johnny, and said, "Here Johnny, here's a picture of the world. It's a puzzle, and if you put the world back together, we will take time to play."

Little Johnny came back three minutes later, with the picture assembled. Shocked, his father said, "That's good Johnny, but how did you do that so fast?"

Little Johnny replied, "It was easy, Daddy! On the other side of the picture of the world was a picture of a mommy, daddy, and their son. When you put the family back together, the world goes back together, too."

Dayle Maloney has given my family and me the opportunity to come back together closer than we have ever been, and it feels wonderful. We are thankful for Dayle, David Bertrand, Jana Mitcham and Nutrition For Life who have made it possible for my family and me to enjoy this wonderful life.

wife, Pam; daughter, Melissa Mercedes, 3; Mike Nadeau

Success Secret ...

"Choose a career you love and you'll
never have to work a day in your life."

PART 4

You *Tell* More Than You *Sell*

What about those people who say, "Oh, no. I can't sell."

Have you ever heard that? It doesn't make sense. When you were 3 years old you couldn't ride a bicycle either. Did your parents say, "Oh, no, no, no! You can't *ever* ride a bicycle. Don't you know that you can't ride?"

When you tried to walk, did they tell you, "Oh, no, no, no! You'll *never* walk."

The truth is we've all got to start somewhere.

You don't have to sell much in this business, you tell — you give people all the information they need to see if this opportunity is for them. People are intelligent enough to know if freedom of time, more money and control over how they live their lives is what they want or not. So give them the audio tape or video tape and let them tell you if it's what they want.

I don't sell much. I share and sample the products with people. How do you share? Samples. Invest $20, $30 or even $100 a month in samples. Our products are consumable

— when the samples are gone, they buy more! <u>I've</u> <u>built</u> <u>my</u> <u>business</u> <u>on</u> <u>samples</u>. Here's a Business Builder's Tip: Give out samples of products that give fast results! I would never give out samples of Oraflow Plus. A person could take that nutritional product for two months and not *feel* any different but it may be working just fine.

So what do I use? Here's a great one. Sunjing Oil. You get 10 sample vials of Sunjing Oil. They're going to feel results with this stuff. I soak in 10-12 drops in my bath water everyday. It *feels* wonderful! It's great for headaches, arthritic relief — and hemorrhoids. (Put two drops, twice a day on the <u>navel</u> for hemorrhoids.)

What else do I sample? Nutri-Cookies. Those cookies taste great. Do you know what's nice about Nutri-Cookies? You can tell who needs them. You don't say, "Hey, you're overweight! You ought to get some cookies."

Instead you walk up and ask, "Have you ever tried our delicious chocolate, chocolate chip cookie?"

"Why no," they answer.

"Well here…" you say as you hand them one of each of the four flavors. They'll find out later it's a weight-loss cookie when they read the wrapper. People love them. I have about 50 customers for a case of cookies each and every month. We don't call them Nutri-Cookies; we call them *fortune cookies*. You can make a *fortune* with those *cookies* if you want to. Most cookie customers will eventually become good distributors.

Give out samples of Pain Relief Plus. This is how I built the business back in 1985. When I went out on the road, I'd always start a meeting by asking, "Is there anyone here tonight who has an ache or pain of any kind?"

Sometimes it was hard to get anybody to fess up, but usually someone would. I'd get them up to the front of the room. I'd always crack open a new bottle and give them two capsules with a glass of fresh water. I'd instruct them to go back and have a seat. Then I would start the meeting. After 30 minutes we asked the person if they felt better.

Friend, traveling all over the country that year, we had over 1,000 people take the test ... two Pain Relief Plus, wait 30 minutes and see if it works. Out of 1,000 people there were only *eight* who didn't feel relief after 30 minutes. It's an incredible product. I built a check of over *$10,000 a month* with the help of Pain Relief Plus. Again, it's fast results.

What else do we use? XL Herbal Energizer and Nutique Skincare Samplers. Nutique is so good I loaned a local distributor two women's kits 5 months ago and now I can't recognize her to get them back. Again fast results.

Another product I use is Nutri-Fiber. You can build any size check you want on this product. We don't get enough fiber in the diet. Take Nutri-Fiber twice a day — morning and night.

I think you know the story of when I got involved June 11, 1985. *I was excited!* Excited but broke. I met David Bertrand and Jana Mitcham and one of their health experts. The doctor said, "I think you're constipated."

I was told I was *constipated* the day I joined this program. But I said I'll never quit! I'll never quit — constipated or not. The doctor said, "Hey, take the test. If you're not constipated the perfect stool will be one inch in diameter and 18 inches long. Two "niners" or three "sixers" would be okay, too."

I said, "Doc, I flunk the test."

He assured me, "You and most everybody else. Just try one container of Nutri-Fiber. In 10 days it should do two things: number one it should put a bounce in your step and a smile on your face; number two it's probably going to make you a charter member of The Perfect Stool Club."

I hit the requirements in 5 days. Great product! Everyone needs to take it. See, I'm trying to make it the number one selling product in this company. It's not. Right now it is the 22nd best seller. I'm failing in my mission. I want to make it the number one seller. It's the number one *mover* ... but it's not the number one *seller*. I need your help! So please buy that Nutri-Fiber.

Success Secret...

"We are paid to generate product volume. Products are the fuel that drives the vehicle called NFLI. Take a product tour of your own home and start buying everything you can from your own store. Products you buy elsewhere — when you could buy them from yourself — are the most expensive products in your home."

PART 5

Do I Know Something
That You Don't Know?

Rita Ambourn, Platinum Executive, Minnesota
Acting On A Good Idea Is Better
Than Just Having A Good Idea

When I received my first bonus check for $253 from Nutrition For Life, I didn't know what it was for. I thought, "The computer made a mistake."

I called the company and they said, "No, that's your retailer's bonus."

I realized I had better look at what I had gotten myself into. I was a "green horn" and didn't have a clue what network marketing was about.

By listening to Dayle Maloney, Kevin Trudeau, and our many other successful leaders, I've become a prosperous Platinum leader whose organization has grown to include several hundred distributors since my enrollment date of January 2, 1996.

I love my Nutrition For Life business so much that it's hard to work it *only* part-time. My full-time effort goes to my nationally acclaimed salon, Rita Ambourn's Hair and Day Spa, in St. Paul, Minnesota. You may wonder, "Rita, if network marketing is so great then why do you only work it part-time?" I have nearly *100 employees* and thousands of customers who have helped me develop the salon to over a $1,500,000.00 business. It requires my full-time effort to maintain. My network marketing business requires only part-time effort to build. I know a time will soon come when my network marketing business will earn more than my salon.

To keep myself healthy with my busy schedule, I've studied nutrition for 18 years and applied what I have learned to my lifestyle. My original reason for joining Nutrition For Life was to purchase better quality products at wholesale prices instead of what I was already buying at retail prices.

Before enrolling in Nutrition For Life, I met with the owner of the health food store where I shopped and asked, "Can I purchase your products at wholesale?"

"No," he informed me.

"Well, can I get a bonus check from you?"

"Well, no," he said, as he looked at me like I had lost my mind.

"Will you give me a free car for the rest of my life?"

"No!" he replied, ready to kick me out of his store.

Giving him one final chance at my business, I asked, "Why should I buy from you? Why wouldn't I buy from my own store?"

He asked me to leave.

It doesn't take a rocket scientist to figure out you should keep your money at home working for you. That's why network marketing is so powerful. You purchase products that you would normally purchase anyway — food, nutritionals, Nightingale-Conant tape programs, hair care and body care ... 400 products — and have others do the same. Then the company sends you a bonus check and provides you the opportunity to earn a free car.

It sounds so simple, doesn't it? Why would anyone start a retail, manufacturing or service business instead of network marketing?

I opened my salon 37 years ago. Back then, store front business owners and employers had better tax advantages, capital was easier to find, and the laws and court system were much fairer to employers and store front business owners. Most people don't have a clue how hard it is to succeed in traditional business today — it's possible, but so few survive. Even as established as my salon is, I still work around the clock to stay competitive — no time off and no relaxing.

When it comes to traditional business, the land of milk and honey is gone. But through network marketing, the American Dream can still be found. Why is network marketing such a great opportunity? For a minimal investment and working only part-time, people can build immediate and residual incomes.

What's residual income? It's a check you receive month-after-month whether you have worked those months or not. An interest check from a savings account is an example of one form of residual income. It is passive income.

I can't — maybe it's that I really don't want to — keep up the same fast-track pace I have for the past 40 years. In a *USA Today* poll, 74% of executives said they would choose a slower career track for more family time. It seems in the 1980's we lived to work. Today, people just want to live.

Because of the success I have received through my day spa and salon, I am interviewed often. When reporters ask me: "Rita, if you had to start your business career all over again, what would you do?"

Every time I answer, "I'd do network marketing."

Their eyes shoot a puzzled look at me: "You're not supposed to say *that*."

Apparently, I know something that they don't know, and now you do, too. The most important step is the first one … enroll today.

Dayle Maloney and Rita Ambourn

Success Secret ...

"Five people you know will join
Nutrition For Life and become
Platinum with or without you!
Which way do you prefer?"

PART 6

It Is Darkest
Before The Dawn

Dori Allibon, 4-Star Platinum Executive, Texas
Try and Try Again

I met Dayle Maloney in 1977 when I was a divisional manager at Rubbermaid where Dayle conducted a *Secrets of Selling Seminar* — this was even before he was in network marketing. Dayle was a wonderful speaker. Afterwards, we spoke and hit it off.

I retired and decided I wanted to start a network marketing business. I knew it was a viable industry and probably the only way an average person could be financially independent and have time freedom. I started with another company because I didn't have any idea Dayle had also gotten involved in the industry.

I joined my first company because of someone's enthusiasm about her company. She made it sound like the best thing since sliced bread. Over a period of 3 ½ years, I tried 9 different companies. Two of them were ground-floor opportunities and, yes, they went into the ground. Then I tried a one-product company which limited me because not everyone is interested in that one product. I tried some of the breakaway companies where only the people at the top make any money. Finally, I became very disgusted with the industry in general.

One day I saw an ad in the paper. It was good ole Dayle Maloney offering the *Secrets Of Multi-Level Marketing Seminar*. I attended and afterwards we spoke. He recommended Nutrition For Life and I trusted his judgement — he became my sponsor. Dayle Maloney is my friend, my mentor, my teacher, my coach; he is just a wonderful sponsor and really a great guy.

Dayle has had an enormous impact on the way business is done in America. We have always known him as Mr. MLM (Multi-Level Marketing). When a person reaches Dayle's stature and position he or she gets noticed — he or she is very prominent and visible. Dayle Maloney is Nutrition For Life and Nutrition For Life is Dayle Maloney. There is also Kevin Trudeau, and we call Dayle and Kevin the "Twin Towers." There are many names coming up now, but for many years Dayle was *THE* name.

Some people who start a network marketing business believe all of a sudden they will have $10,000 in their account the next day — that really doesn't happen. It takes a while to build. People who move product volume by sponsoring a good number of people quickly are going to make good money, but it takes time to build the long-term residual income.

My business grew slowly and steadily. Each month my check grows larger. The true reward is the long-term residual income. It stays there even if I stop sponsoring or retire and just purchase products.

Dayle is the most caring, loving individual I know. He wouldn't have to reach back and help the people that haven't made it, but he does. Dayle feels pleasure from helping other people and the people mean more to him than the money — that's the kind of guy Dayle is — not out for the almighty buck.

When Dayle and I were in Miami together, I arranged a meeting for a prospect to meet Dayle. My prospect didn't show. Dayle just took it in stride and laughed, "That one's a no-show." Later, I called my prospect and asked him if he was out of his mind. I told him, "Wow! People would do most anything to have a private meeting with Dayle Maloney."

In the last year I've been in what is called the management mode — trying to manage the people in my organization. It made me stagnant. What I am doing now is sponsoring. When you want to put excitement into your group, SPONSOR! People follow the leader.

Dayle gives good advice: "No matter what the problem or challenge is, just go out and sponsor somebody new."

Dori Allibon
4-Star Platinum Executive, Texas

Success Secret...

"Success is just failure turned inside out. When you feel like quitting, that's when you've almost made it."

PART 7

Enthusiasm is Highly Contagious

Sheryl Wong, 4-Star Platinum Executive, Hawaii
Enthusiasm And Confidence Are
Great Business Building Tools In Any Economy

I was looking for diversification of income. I was not looking for a network marketing business because I was the typical skeptic who thought they were all scams.

I knew plenty of doctors, realtors, retailers, and corporate executives who succeeded in their fields, but I did not know too many people who had developed successful careers in network marketing. I thought network marketing was only for desperate people who had no other choices in life. I didn't believe it was for people who could achieve professional success.

I am a successful realtor. When I was approached with Nutrition For Life in 1995, the real estate market in Hawaii was on a downswing and my commission checks became very sporadic. I was approached with an audio tape which educated me on how Nutrition For Life was different from other network marketing companies.

I agreed to give it a try but I did so using the poke-it-with-a-stick method. I found myself a business partner, Cammie Yee, and my initial investment of time and money was half the risk.

I didn't approach too many people, and those I did, it was just half heartily. Our first two weeks, we sponsored eight executives. Our first check was almost $3,000. "Wow!" No liability, no employees, no boss, free advertising — I took a closer look. From that time, with persistence and tenacity, we built a 4-Star Platinum business. Now that I have a taste of network marketing — I can't beat it. Nothing else can match what network marketing can provide.

Sheryl Wong, 4-Star Platinum Executive, Hawaii

Success Secret ...

"You can't excite people if *you* are not excited."

PART 8

The Dayle Maloney I Know

Louie & May Abude, Gold Executives, California
Being Friends With "One Of The Greats"

In 1994, ten years after I first met Dayle, I saw an ad he was running in *USA Today* for a network marketing opportunity. I called the ad. After ten years, Dayle still remembered my original address in Alameda, California and my real first name (my former name was Lorenzio).

Dayle said, "Fly on down to Orange County, and I would like to put you up in a hotel. You and your wife will be my guests." He treated us like royalty for the next 3 days. Dayle introduced us to the leadership of Nutrition For Life: President David Bertrand, Executive Vice-President Jana Mitcham, Wes Spiegel, and the local California leaders. When we saw the type of people involved, we became very interested in the company.

David and Jana were down-to-earth, very humble people. Together they told May and me, "We created Nutrition For Life for the distributors and they come first." I believe that is why David and Jana are always out in the field.

When May and I were ready to leave the rally in Orange County, we hugged Dayle in the hallway. He gave me a box of business building tools and said, "Louie, don't ever learn how to quit." Dayle Maloney has imbedded those words into my subconscious mind. No matter how challenging any area of my life becomes, those words keep ringing in my mind.

My friendship with Dayle has changed my life. I want to walk in his shoes and pass the legacy on to my family, my associates, and whomever I meet.

Dayle Maloney has a big heart and this is why he is a legend. Dayle brilliantly remembers the little things. There are 60,000 people in Dayle's downline — and he knows most of them — but he always sends me a present every Christmas. I tell my distributors, "Here's a guy who knows the world, but he takes the time to write a note and send a present to let you know he is thinking about you."

Recently, I asked Dayle, "How does it feel to be so well known and make all that money?"

Dayle's response was, "Awe Louie, it's all past that. It is the people's lives we touch that counts."

Dayle teaches that it is not just the dream you attain, but the person you become as a result of your trials and tribulations. In this business, you can touch so many lives — like Dayle has done with us. He has made a lasting impression on my life. When I share this story with people, they can see why with this kind of leadership the company is so successful. It has been a tremendously successful experience, and I will always stay loyal to this company.

May & Louie Abude and family

Success Secret ...

"One of the most important responsibilities of a leader is to eliminate his or her people's excuses for defeat."

PART 9

If You're Not Having Fun, You're In The Wrong Business

Patrick and Christine Carr, Platinum Executives, Illinois
You'll Be In Business For Yourself,
But Not By Yourself

When Dayle Maloney turned 60, we gave him a birthday card which read, "Now that you've turned 60, are you going to slow down enough to let the rest of us catch up with you?" If you know Dayle, you know that fits him perfectly — he doesn't know what "idle" is.

When we first entered this industry, it was in another network marketing company. We had a prospect who wanted to meet our upline to make sure they were strong so we put them in touch, and our upline sponsored them — they had stolen our prospect! Obviously, the upline lost all credibility with us.

They realized after it was all done, they made a major mistake but we couldn't overcome our shock. My wife, Chris, and I started looking around for another company. A year earlier, when we were researching the industry, we answered Dayle Maloney's ad in the *USA Today*. He sent us a cassette tape. We listened to the cassette tape and it was so powerful that we really thought about joining, but at the time, we were happy with our other program. We decided to keep this cassette tape on file ... just in case.

When our upline stole our prospect, we asked ourselves, "Remember the tape we listened to a year ago? Where is it?" We truly tore our house apart for three days searching for the tape because the label contained Dayle's phone number.

I called Dayle and explained we had a little over 100 people in our downline. I told him we wanted to be in business with someone we trusted who would help us grow.

He assured me, "Well, you've found it."

I questioned him, "Yeah, everyone and their brother tells me that. What are you going to do that is different? How are you going to help us as our upline?"

"I'll do whatever I can," he replied.

"Would you be able to do a meeting? I'm in Chicago ... you're up in Eau Claire," I wondered out loud.

"Yeah, I'd do a meeting for you," he said.

I'm thinking, "Yeah, right," so I asked, "Okay, when?"

I heard the pages of his planner rustling as he asked, "How about a week from Thursday?"

I couldn't believe it! I jumped, "Okay, I'm in!" We joined that day in August, 1993 and Dayle came down a week from the following Thursday and held a meeting for us at our house to launch our business.

It was apparent Dayle believed we could succeed. When we hit tough times, he was always an open ear for us, always a source of motivation. We cannot remember a single conversation or telephone call we've had with him where we didn't feel 100 times more motivated. He has always been a positive influence in our lives, and Chris and I thank God we've had the opportunity to work with him.

Dayle is one of our closest friends. We can look him in the eye and truly say, "We love you!"

Patrick Carr having a great time posing for a picture
with Dayle Maloney and Nutrition For Life
4-Star Executive, Dori Allibon.

Success Secret ...

"Success is getting what you want.
Happiness is wanting what you get."

PART 10

We Loved Network Marketing But Couldn't Make Enough Money Until...

Jack And Jody Lundie,
4-Star Platinum Executives, Kansas
Making Money In Network Marketing

We were disillusioned with our network marketing company prior to Nutrition For Life but we *loved* the time freedom it gave us. We knew people made money in network marketing, but we were struggling with our previous company trying to create the kind of life *financially* that we wanted.

When you approach network marketers who are struggling in their company, once you show them what Nutrition For Life has in place, it's a no-brainer.

We are not talking about stealing people from other companies. If someone is succeeding in another network marketing company — we have no business talking to them about joining our company. This business is about getting to know other people. There are plenty of people who have not heard of Nutrition For Life.

There are *other* good network marketing companies out there. We personally feel Nutrition For Life is the best, but we would hope people in the industry are loyal to their company — if their company is treating them right.

Now down the road, if they have become disenchanted with their company, then a relationship has been built. At that point, you can talk to them about an opportunity with Nutrition For Life.

Dayle has taught us to always share this opportunity with everyone. It may or may not be for them.   Dayle teaches us not to run down the other companies. He instructs us to just show people what we have, keep their name on file and check back with them six   months or so later. People's situations change.

Some people will put you to the test and say, "Let's see if you're going to be with that company in *another* six months." They're amazed to see not only are you *with* the company but you're *more excited* about the business a year or two years later than when you started.

To succeed you must find a company that treats you well.   In this industry what does that mean? The company must provide their distributors with the basics for success: offer consumable products people want, pay you on time, ship orders promptly, publicly recognize achievement and offer a simple, easy, duplicable business building system.

With our prior network marketing company we had only 5 people in our organization who were excited enough to go out and show the plan.   When people aren't excited, your business becomes a sales job. We kept sponsoring people but nobody else wanted to do anything — the company didn't give them a reason to.

We made the decision we were going to contact most of our people one-on-one and that's exactly what we did. It seems like it takes longer. It really doesn't.

We schedule an initial 20 minute meeting with the goal to have them agree to look at the sponsoring video tape or listen to one of the audio tapes — depending if they have a drive ahead of them and can listen to an audio or would rather watch a video. The initial appointment is to convey the excitement, build up the industry, inform them why *we* are building a network marketing business and why *other people* are becoming involved. We just say to them, "This is exciting! Let's do this together." The rest they can learn from the video or the audios.

What is the best piece of advice we can give a new Nutrition For Life distributor? Don't stop sponsoring! When our organization's growth exploded, we shifted from a sponsoring mode to a management mode. We worried too much about our downline and spent too much time trying to manage them. If we had just kept sponsoring 3 or 4 people a month since day one, instead of taking a year off from sponsoring, we'd probably be at our next achievement level which is 5-Star Platinum instead of 4-Star Platinum.

There is nothing more exciting for you or your group than having a new personally sponsored executive. A new person adds new excitement. Looking back, we should have spent less time being motivators. People are motivated by what you do! If our organization had the opportunity to watch us continue to sponsor, there would have been more sponsoring by everyone. We would have built a larger and more secure business *quicker*.

I don't think there is anyone who cares more about

Nutrition For Life and its people than Dayle Maloney. I think he's *everybody's hero.*

See, Jody and I were just *regular* people and we were able to make it big in Nutrition For Life. We look at Dayle and he gives us a lot of hope.

Dayle is succeeding incredibly with a solid *6-figure, monthly income* and he's <u>not</u> a doctor or somebody who knew one or two people he could sponsor who would bring in millions of people. Instead, he went *out* and *met* a million people and that's so *impressive* to us. He was an average guy who did the things most people are afraid to do.

Dayle came from the type of background a lot of people came from and wished they could make it — but fear they can't. Dayle is <u>living</u> <u>proof</u> *they can.* Dayle is an <u>everyday</u> <u>person</u> who *made it big.* He had *everything* going against him and is successful only because *he did not give up.* He kept going and going and going — like the Energizer Bunny.

Dayle had many strikes against him: his health has been bad, he was piled in debt, no college degree, no family money, no business contacts, no job, homeless at 47. But, he didn't let anything stand in his way. Dayle is *proof* anyone can succeed in this business.

Through all the success, Dayle still remembers the people. How many successful businessmen will take time for children? When Dayle calls our house and our 9-year old son, Murphy, answers he talks with our son longer than he talks with us. Murphy *waits* with excitement for Dayle to call.

Dayle Maloney is in this *for the people.* He cares about everybody so much. He is a true leader because he has brought out in thousands of people's hearts their desires to help others succeed.

**Jack and Jody Lundie have 3 sons:
Jeremiah, 18, Jacob, 17, and Murphy, 9.**

Success Secret ...

"You can make more friends in two
months by becoming interested in
others than you can in two years by
trying to make others interested in you."

PART 11

All It Takes Is One

Jean Worden, Platinum Executive, Oregon
To Succeed You Start At The Beginning

When I first started in Nutrition For Life in 1989, Dayle agreed to host two days of meetings for me in my home in Oregon. A week before the meeting Dayle called, "Jean, I can save $343 on my plane ticket if we start the meeting at 7:00 at night instead of at 1:00 that afternoon."

I replied, "Dayle, I've got all these people coming ... I've invited 100 people."

He comforted me: "Okay, Jean, I'll be there at 1 o'clock."

Sure enough, he came. We met in my home where we were holding the meeting, and after sizing up the crowd, I said, "Dayle, we only have three people at the meeting, and one of them is me." You can imagine how I felt — three people out of 100 for two days' worth of meetings.

He said in a motivating manner, "Don't worry, Jean. We'll have a good meeting. All it takes is one." Dayle presented that meeting as though I had all 100 people in the room. It was wonderful. The next day, we had 15-20 people.

Dayle was back in Albany, Oregon six months later with David and Jana and we had 130 people at a hotel meeting. He was right — it only takes one!

I have worked with David Bertrand, Jana Mitcham, and Dayle Maloney for over 8 years now. They impress me just as much today as when they were in my living room helping me build my business. Dayle is a super person who has earned respect from thousands of people because he has always been there for them.

Dayle is the example of what it takes to make it in network marketing. He tells you to never, never quit. Even though he is a multi-millionaire, Dayle is still out there working the business. You look up to people like that.

Jean Worden
Platinum Executive, Oregon

Success Secret ...

"The secret to building a successful downline is not sponsoring thousands of people *yourself*. Rather, it is developing and training the *people* you already have sponsored — so *together* you can sponsor thousands of people."

Special Introduction
To Chapter 7

Author's Note:

Why would I make a special introduction to Chapter 7?

Because what you are holding in your hands is so powerful, I want to make sure I have your attention. The marketing secrets which are about to be revealed to you may seem so easy or simple — at times foolishly simple — that you might not believe they work.

Read what Larry McClain has to say about Dayle's marketing techniques and you will see Dayle's secrets are time-tested. Dayle's techniques were first proven in the recreational vehicle industry. How well do they transfer to network marketing? Dayle has enjoyed success in both industries using these techniques. How? Human wants, needs and desires remain the same.

So sit back and enjoy as Larry shares with you the colorful history of Dayle Maloney's marketing techniques.

The Ice Cream Man

Larry McClain, Founder and CEO, McClain's RV Superstores, Inc.

Author's Note: Larry McClain is Founder and Chief Executive Officer of McClain's RV Superstores, Inc. with retail locations in Dallas, Fort Worth and two locations in Oklahoma City. I asked Larry to give us some insight on what Dayle Maloney was like before his success in network marketing. In the 1960's, Dayle worked for Apache Camping Trailers helping and motivating dealers in the field.

In 1964, as a 24-year old, wet-behind-the-ears, undercapitalized entrepreneur, I placed a few Apache campers on a 75' x 80' gravel lot in Oklahoma City and called it McClain's RV Campsite. It was my first recreational vehicle dealership. I had no idea what I had gotten myself into, but I had a dream and prayed I would make it.

It was a warm, mid-week afternoon in 1966 when Dayle pulled up on my lot. My heart raced because I thought he was a prospect, and my bank account said I needed to make a sale ... fast.

If Dayle had only bought a camper he would have fed me that day ... instead, he taught me how to sell, and I fed myself and my family for a lifetime.

I was just a novice. My one employee, Gary Motley, and I had a few trailers popped up on the lot and sold them the best way we could. Dayle was sent by the headquarters of Apache Camping Trailers to help us promote and increase revenues. On that fateful visit, I was introduced to promotional marketing at its best.

Dayle showed us powerful simple secrets on how to display our campers. He had us position the most elaborate camper in a certain area of the lot so the families would gravitate to it and experience the comforts of our high-end model. He then had us place our economy units out by the roadside with the prices displayed in big and bold print.

What happened? It was like someone turned on the faucet. The inexpensive price pulled the families in, and Mom and Dad spent the additional money to purchase the comforts of the upscale models. My luck and the balance in my bank account began to change.

Dayle wrote promotional ads for us. They were different from the basic "who-what-where" ads we were running. He added hot prices, exciting events and deadlines to everything so there would be a "sense-of-urgency": "This weekend only!" or "For 5 days only!"

Today, this may be old news to you, but remember this all happened back in 1966 — before Dayle's techniques became the norm.

Dayle came in one Saturday about 9 a.m. ready to start the day. He was placing several half-gallon containers of ice cream in the freezer compartment of the refrigerator in my office. I asked, "What in the world are you doing? Is all that ice cream for us?"

"No," he said. "We 're going to give this away."

"What?" I questioned. I was sure Maloney had gone too far this time.

He said, "You watch me."

Dayle was just awesome to watch out on the lot among the people. He was masterful at handling groups of people — had them smiling, laughing, and happy to be there. People *wanted* to buy from Dayle. They'd drive off the lot with a new trailer or at least leave a deposit. No one left empty-handed.

When the first family who didn't purchase from Dayle was ready to leave the lot, Dayle said, "Here, let me give you some ice cream to take home with you and enjoy."

After they left, Dayle turned to me and said , "Now, you see what's going to happen? That ice cream is going to melt if they don't go right on home. That'll keep them from stopping and shopping at other dealerships."

We called those the "Days of Dayle." Since that time, our industry has become very promotionally-minded. There is hardly a time I don't think of Dayle Maloney and the secrets he taught me.

Dayle's promotions sold more Apaches for us during the short time he was in Oklahoma than we had sold in our *entire* first two years in business. In 1969, my salesperson, Gary Motley, sold more Apache Campers than any other salesperson in the United States. Dayle helped develop this young man's sales skills and we used whatever promotions Dayle recommended.

My wife, kids and I really needed the financial salvation Dayle created. I know plenty of other dealers whose families benefited from him in those tough, tough, days. We all fought over Dayle because we knew when he arrived, our sales would go through the roof. He taught us techniques in such a way that when he left, we could duplicate what he did.

People loved Dayle because he was genuine and believable. Even today, when we hire salespeople we measure their abilities using Dayle Maloney as the ruler. We are always looking to hire clones of Dayle Maloney.

Last year, McClain's RV Superstores, Inc. grossed in the neighborhood of $75,000,000.00. Today, we offer everything from little fold-up campers to big diesel motor homes.

To think it all started on a gravel lot with a dream, a prayer and a half-gallon of ice cream.

Larry McClain, Founder and CEO
McClain's RV Superstores, Inc.

Success Secret ...

"The greatness of the leader is determined by the strength of their belief, the height of their ambition, the extent of their vision and the magnitude of their love. "

Chapter 7

If You Aren't Plugged In — You Can't Get Turned On

PART 1

Make Or Break Your Business In The First 30 Days

Important notice from Dayle Maloney: Please counsel with your upline if you read about any techniques that you are currently not using. These are simply ideas I have used over the years to build my business, but you must always check upline to see if they fit your organization.

My largest sponsoring month was 164 people. In reality, I wasn't sponsoring them; I was throwing mud against the wall seeing if anyone stuck. We're not concerned about how many you can sponsor. What is important is how many you can sponsor *and* get <u>them</u> <u>started</u> so *they* can duplicate and sponsor people who do the same. When you sponsor your new distributor, **the guidance they receive in the first 30 days** will make or break their business. When they succeed, you succeed.

Ivan Barickman in Minneapolis, is a prime example. Ivan started with Nutrition For Life in 1995 and has personally sponsored only about 15-18 people. Today, Ivan has an organization of distributors numbering in the thousands and a five-figure monthly check.

=====

Success Secret ...

"The Master Developer Series, functions, books and tapes will train your people. It is your responsibility to make sure the people who want to succeed in your organization participate in the training."

=====

PART 2

Building The Business Achieving The Dream

Friend, I believe you have to start your new distributors immediately on the books and tapes and get them attending the functions. Books, tapes and functions are the system. This is how you and your people will learn to build the business and achieve the dream. I believe everyone has to become a book worm and a tape worm. Successful Nutrition For Life distributors learn from the Master Developer Series. It is the best investment you can make in your business and yourself. The training comes from Nightingale-Conant, Distributor Services and Nutrition For Life.

The system makes a novice look good because it multiplies your efforts and creates an environment of success.

Books and tapes are attitude food. Don't ever starve the mind. Do you understand what happens to your mind when the withdrawals outnumber the deposits? When you read books and listen to tapes, you deposit knowledge and information into your mind.

Think about the people who are going to cost you

withdrawals. You hold a meeting and your prospect is a no-show. What happens? Withdrawal, withdrawal, withdrawal.

Somebody says, "No!"

You panic, "Oh Lord, they said 'no' to me." Withdrawal, withdrawal, withdrawal. Please don't count "no's," because "no's" don't count anyway.

If you don't put information and knowledge from books, tapes and functions in your mind, you're going to get *overdrawn*. When you get overdrawn in the mind, then you're going to have the <u>hardest</u> challenge of your life.

You've got to be *in control* of what is fed into your mind. If you're not careful what goes in there, you're probably allowing other people to deposit their information in your mind. What kind of thoughts do you suppose most people will deposit? Positive or negative?

Once positive information enters your mind it is converted into the knowledge your brain uses to function.

Negative knowledge produces fear. Fear produces procrastination. Procrastination produces hunger. Like the one dream stealer said, "I'm not ready to procrastinate, yet." I asked another dream stealer, "I hear you have a problem making a decision." His answer, "Well, yes and no."

Positive knowledge produces confidence. Confidence produces activity. Activity produces results ... I guarantee it!

Realize, you're not spending money when you purchase books, tapes, and function tickets. You're *investing* money in yourself — the finest investment you'll ever make. You have a multi-million dollar computer called the brain.

What's in that brain can never be copied.

From your neck on down you have nothing but the foundation holding up your computer. Think about it, you feed the foundation three times a day. How often do you feed your multi-million dollar computer? When you read books, attend functions, and listen to tapes, you are feeding your computer.

Success Secret ...

"Life is the experience of becoming."

PART 3

Dreams Don't Work
Unless You Do

We have to help newly sponsored people avoid early face-to-face rejection. Why? Let's say you sponsored Joe. He can't wait to go right to the brother-in-law. The brother-in-law says, "Joe, you stupid fool! You got in a pyramid deal!" Joe comes back to you and asks, "Can I get my $49 back and return my products?" You see, Joe didn't seek advice from a graduate — he talked to a drop out.

I spoke at a meeting one night in Central Wisconsin. There was a young woman attending with two little kids whose husband drove a truck. She worked midnight to 8 a.m. somewhere making boxes. She was trying to find a way to make some extra money so someday they could buy a house.

She got involved that night. "I can't wait to get to work at midnight! I'll enroll the whole shift by morning," she exclaimed. This gal was charged up!

Two weeks later, I was speaking at the meeting in that same town. Here she came with her starter kit. The people she worked with had *made fun of her*. "Oh, you got in one of those deals, you fool," they said.

She wanted her money back. My heart broke for her and her two little ones at home. I said, "Oh, we'll get your money back. Why are you letting those people steal your new home — your dream? Why don't you go out and call on total strangers?"

Many times total strangers are easier to present the opportunity to than friends, neighbors and relatives. I don't know about you, but some of my relatives are stinkin' thinkers. Let me tell you. Wow, can't it get ripe around them? Most relatives make *good practice*. They'll shoot all the bad things at you.

If you've got stinkin', thinkin' relatives you may want to make up a master relative list: name, address, city, state, zip, phone number. Then go to another good downline distributor and swap relative lists. You work their relatives and they'll work yours. I've seen it work well for years now. You see, grass is always greener in the next yard, but remember it still has to be cut.

Anyway, this gal agreed to go call on strangers. Now, I don't usually believe in luck. I think luck is really spelled w-o-r-k. The harder you work — the luckier you're going to get. I think she was a little lucky.

She went out and talked to strangers and sponsored 10 people. Four of them started to build their businesses and she earned a check for $800.

I was back in Central Wisconsin for another

opportunity meeting. The entire midnight shift took up one side of the room! They're *all* getting in! I walked over to a big guy and asked, "Hey, are you getting involved?"

"You bet," he barked with excitement.

I inquired, "What made you decide to get involved tonight?"

"I got in because I want to get a check like this gal got the other day," he confessed.

See, they are dream stealers to start with. Go work on strangers if that's your problem. Start making some money and those dream stealers will *all* come on board. That's were it's at.

Success Secret ...

"I believe in luck. The harder I work, the more luck I have."

PART 4

You'll Never Be Remembered For Your Failures, Only For Your Successes

I want you to remember one thing about failure. The only time failure ever counts is if it's the last time you're ever going to try. I've had so many failures, I can't even put them all down in this book today — *there aren't enough pages*!

You get up and you just keep on going. You will never be remembered for your failures, only your successes. You understand, in northern Wisconsin I had three little, small town banks close my checking accounts — too much month left at the end of the money. Everyone in those towns knew it.

But I go up there today and they get all excited: "Oh, that guy made millions!" They forget about failures. Don't you ever worry about it. When you've failed, don't concentrate on the failure — that's history and you can't change it. Instead, concentrate on your dream. That's the future and you can create it.

You're going to have some failures. It just happens. My favorite story is about Thomas Edison. You see, he invented the light bulb on the 1,064th attempt. He was asked by a young reporter, "Oh, Mr. Edison, how could you stand to fail 1,063 times?"

He looked puzzled at the young man and said, "I never failed once. I simply invented 1,063 ways the bulb would not light."

If you want to succeed, that's how you look at failure. Failure is nothing but an event.

• Walt Disney was turned down by 302 bankers trying to borrow $50,000 to start a movie production company. I'm glad he kept on going. We might not have had Mickey Mouse or Donald Duck.

• Babe Ruth was the all time leader in strikeouts in major league baseball. He struck out many times for every time he hit a home run, but we only remember him as the King of Swat — hitting home runs.

• In the 1870's, Alexander Graham Bell invented the telephone. President Hayes, after making a test call, said, "That's an amazing invention, but who would ever want one of them?"

• Dr. Robert Schuller always said it's better to try something and fail than do nothing and succeed.

• Elvis Presley was fired after his debut appearance at the Grand Ole Opry in 1954. Jimmy Denny, Opry manager, told Elvis, "You ain't going nowhere, son. You ought go back to drivin' truck."

• Abraham Lincoln was demoted from Captain to Private during the Blackhawk War.

• When Marilyn Monroe was starting out in 1944, a modeling agency owner told her she lacked beauty and talent. The owner recommended that Marilyn's only life hope was to find a husband to support her or learn to type.

• Florence Joyner, nick-named "FloJo," practiced for ten years to shave one second off her time in the 100 meter dash so she could win an Olympic Gold medal.

• Olympic Gold Medalist, Wilma Rudolph, was born prematurely. By age 4, double pneumonia and scarlet fever had left one of her legs paralyzed. By 13, she was able to hobble without a leg brace. She started entering races, finishing last for many years. People told her to give it up. All the years paid off when she won her first race. From that point on, Wilma won them all. Wilma, who at age 9 was told she'd never walk without braces, won 3 Olympic Gold medals. It takes patience to continually improve.

"My mother taught me very early to believe I could achieve any accomplishment I wanted to. The first was to walk without braces."

Wilma Rudolph

We just remember success.

Success Secret ...

"To become successful, people must win a quiet victory within — self-discipline comes before success."

PART 5

Succeed By Doing Common Things Well

I like positive goals but I'm going to give you *one negative* goal. When you put this book down today, hit the ground running, and in the next few months try to have <u>100 people</u> say, "No!" to you in Nutrition For Life. Write the names of 100 people you showed the plan to who told you, "No!" You'll be very successful before you reach that goal of 100 "no's." The toughest "no's" — the ones who ridicule you and make fun of you — go on your "in-spite-of-list." You'll build this business to get revenge on those folks.

Don't get in the habit of expecting "no's." Remember, you don't get recognition or checks for *just showing* the plan, —you have to sponsor people into the business.

Go out and show the plan in a *true attempt* to sponsor them in the business. But keep working towards your goal of 100 "no's." Remember, after a certain number of "no's," you'll get a "Yes." The "yes's" put you well on your way to big checks and recognition.

Success Secret ...

"You get more out of life by trying something and failing than you do by trying nothing and succeeding."

PART 6

Avoiding Face-To-Face Rejection

Who are your best prospects? People you know on a first name basis. You have to keep a prospect list and add names to it every day.

Don't ever pre-judge prospects. There are only two ways prospects ever get off your prospect list. Number one is when they enroll and start their Nutrition For Life business — cross them off the prospect list. The other way? When you pick up the local newspaper and read their obituary — take them off. Other than that they stay on your list.

When I sponsor a brand new person, I have them make up a list of 100 people they know on a first name basis, immediately. This is called S-O-U, Sense Of Urgency. My new enrollee sends a half page letter to the people on his or her list within 24-hours, saying that they and their family have found a fantastic opportunity and they'd like to share it.

Month Day, Year

Dear (Insert Prospect's Name),

We found a great family business opportunity and we'd love to share it with you. We're sure excited about it, and we think you'd be excited, too. If you want to hear more about it, (Insert Prospect's Name), there's no obligation and no charge. Send back the bottom half of this letter and I'll send you the information.

Sincerely,

(Your Name)

(Have the bottom half of this letter be a fill-in-the-blank form where your prospects indicate their name, address, phone number and best time to call.)

By today's standards, it's going to cost about $50 to $75 to mail 100 letters including envelopes, copies, and postage. Usually anywhere from 5 to 15 of your friends will send back the bottom half — if even just out of courtesy or friendship.

Here's the key. Your new enrollee will receive the responses. They'll call you like they've won the Powerball Lottery and scream, "I can't believe it! Fourteen people want to hear about Nutrition For Life."

See, 86 people said, "No" to your new enrollee,

wrinkled him or her up, tossed them aside into the wastebasket. Not one of those rejections was face-to-face. It's a great confidence builder.

Now, you've got to take charge and help your new enrollee meet two-on-one with those 14 people if they are local. Normally, your enrollee's list is going to be local people as most times our distributors build their business locally. Remember, please go across the street before you go down the street. Your best prospects are in the block where you live. If the prospect is not local, simply use three-way calling.

For building a solid network marketing organization, we use a technique called a "tap root." It's our goal to "tap" the "roots" of our new enrollees' organizations three-levels deep by working with their warm market to sponsor people. We help our enrollees' new enrollees sponsor people until our personal enrollees have people on their first three levels. During this process we are setting a tradition of how future organizations are to be built.

What's the result of the "tap root" system?

You sponsor Sue. Help Sue sponsor Paul. Help Paul sponsor Diane. Help Diane sponsor Joe. Now Sue's downline is tapped three levels deep with Paul, Diane, and Joe. Odds are the organization is solid and will never unravel.

Each time you coach a new enrollee to write their prospect list of 100 people who they know on a first name basis, you are increasing your organization's potential for success. Where at first you were only tapping into your warm market, now you have many other folks in your organization whose warm market can be contacted.

Success Secret ...

"In network marketing your income is based on more than sponsoring people from *your* prospect list. It is based on helping your people succeed in sponsoring people from *their* prospect lists, and helping your people's people succeed in sponsoring from *their* prospect lists and so on."

PART 7

Sizing Up Your Odds For Success

When you sponsor 10 new enrollees and three or four of them aggressively build the business, rejoice! If one out of 10 builds, rejoice! As long as people occupy a position in your organization and buy product every month — that's okay. You are paid on product movement. Remember, in network marketing you have to continually sponsor new people.

Why don't all new enrollees go out and build their businesses? Because of worry. Some people worry about what their friends, neighbors and relatives are going to think. You've seen this happen. Somebody says to them, "What do you do?"

You overhear you distributor reply, "Well it's kind of a little advertising thing, kind of word-of-mouth. Oh, we have some products." They are worried.

My wife, Jeannine, used to worry like that but has gotten over it ... she ought to — it's been 15 years.

Jeannine and I were on an all-expenses-paid company 3-day cruise a few years ago with a group of Nutrition For Life distributors. We met two couples from Iowa who had won their cruise in a grocery store drawing. I sized them up as pretty good prospects. We were just beginning our conversation with them when Jim Leyde, a real leader in my organization, tapped me on the shoulder. As I was standing with my back to Jeannine and the group, talking to Leyde, I overheard the conversation Jeannine was having with the two couples. They asked my wife, "Say, what *is* it that your husband does?"

Jeannine responded shortly, "Well you have to ask him about that."

That was a few years ago. Jeannine's a lot more comfortable today about the business.

The bottom line is — why worry? Only eight out of 100 things you worry about ever come true. Only four of the eight ever turn out badly. Why lose sleep when only four of 100 *might* turn out negative.

To me worry is interest on a debt that may never come due.

Friend, another reason people may not build their businesses is called a *sense of unworthiness*. It is foolish. You meet people daily who don't think they are worthy of success. "Oh, I'm not interested. I couldn't do that," they say.

They've lost the dream or have had it stolen. They don't think they can succeed. We have to recapture those people and get them dreaming again.

Hey, you are already wealthy. I'm not saying you've cashed in yet, but you are wealthy. Imagine this, if you live in North America and *even if* you are on welfare, you are still in the top 5% standard of living anywhere in the world. You're wealthy.

I'll prove it to you right here. Would you sell your two eyes for a million bucks? Would you sell your two ears for a million bucks? How about your two arms and your two legs, a package deal, for a million? I never get a taker.

Well, if your eyes are worth a million, your ears a million, arms and legs ... well, you're already worth $3,000,000.00 — you just haven't cashed in yet.

You are worthy of success! Stand in front of a mirror everyday and look yourself straight in the eyes and say, "Why not me and why not now?" I do a lot of mirror sayings.

Something else you want to ask yourself every night before you go to sleep, "How much money would I have made today if my downline did what I did?" If you're embarrassed by the answer, you better work a little harder tomorrow. If you are ever thinking of quitting, here is a "mirror-saying" for you: "Faith that fizzles before the finish was faulty from the first."

Don't worry about network marketing. Nutrition For Life is the last frontier of free enterprise. This is a 100% equal opportunity business — your pay is based on your efforts, not your seniority.

Success Secret ...

"You have a power inside of you which is greater than any obstacle which lies before you — will power."

PART 8

Sponsor Up!

When it comes to sponsoring new enrollees, always seek people at your ambition level and above. That technique is called sponsoring up. Sponsoring people at less than your ambition level is called sponsoring down. Don't pass on anyone — if they are breathing and can fog a mirror, sponsor them, but concentrate on sponsoring up.

Likewise, "associate up" with people. If you want to make money in network marketing, hang around people who are making money in the business. The other day, a guy told me, "I want to make $100,000 a year in this company."

I think he was serious about it, but do you know what he did? He talked to his brother-in-law who can't even pay his bills about how to make $100,000 a year.

You must seek advice from the graduates *not* the drop outs. There are lots of drop-outs in this world. Their advice isn't worth 5 cents for 24-hours, friend. Don't listen to those people unless you want to be one of them. Seek advice up — not down.

Success Secret ...

"Discouragement is a test of your character — to see what, if anything, it takes to stop you."

PART 9

When You're Down, Call Up

Avoid calling your downline when you are down or upset. It's a mistake most of us in the network marketing industry have made.

If your bonus check drops, somebody quits, or somebody says, "No" — those are NEVER the times to call the downline. I've got a guy in my group who recently called two leaders in his organization and dumped on them. Stupidity is what it is because he took the excitement out of their hearts. Excitement is the fuel we need to sponsor people. Don't ever strip the people in your organization of excitement.

When you're *down* — call the upline. When you're *up* — call the downline. You know my reasoning? When you're sick — you throw up, you don't throw down! That's one of the most important things you'll read on these pages. Never call down when you are down.

Success Secret ....

"Motivation is the cornerstone to success. You can *do* the work of more than one person, but you can't *be* more than one person. You must inspire *your* people to inspire *their* people."

PART 10

You Are One Good Question Away From Your Fortune

A while back I presented a home-based business seminar in Winona, Minnesota, a beautiful river town. I asked the crowd if there was anyone in the audience who owned a store front business. A man raised his hand. I asked, "Sir, what type of business do you own?"

"A barber shop across the river in Alma, Wisconsin," he proudly informed me. He said his name was Dave.

I inquired, "Dave, what's the price of a hair cut?"

"Nine bucks," he quoted me.

"Wow, cheap, nine bucks up here, huh?" I continued, "Dave, if you had a customer waiting at the door when you opened in the morning and you had them lined up for haircuts all day long, how many heads of hair could you cut in a full day?"

"Well, probably 25 to 30," he figured.

"Have you ever cut that many in a day?" I wondered out loud.

"Well, no," he said disappointingly.

"What do you usually cut?" I asked.

"About 10-15," he confided.

Well in this situation, even if Dave could cut at his maximum output of 30 heads of hair at $9 each, his income is still limited. In this case, the most money he could ever earn is $270 a day. Dave has to pay rent, utilities, advertising — he's got everything to pay for out of the $270. And there's no residual income.

So I asked, "Dave, would you be interested in increasing your revenue with no extra overhead?" There's the *key phrase*. Friend, if you use this phrase, nine out of 10 store-front owners will look at what you've got. It's just that simple.

Start contacting one store-front merchant everyday. You may want to leave them a video. If they haven't got time for a video, then leave them a cassette. Your business will explode simply by calling on one store front merchant everyday.

Who are the best store-front merchants? Small restaurant owners, beauty salon owners and small saloon keepers. They know their entire customer base by their *first names*. You get the right saloon keeper, and he or she will sponsor one person a day for at least 60 days. Believe me it can happen! How? We have to *go to* our warm market. Their warm market *comes to them*.

I don't know for sure why, but we're getting a lot of franchise owners coming into our business. Most franchises leave something to be desired. I believe the people who make money in franchises are the ones who sell them, not the ones who buy them. How do I know? I was the youngest owner of a Dairy Queen at age 18. This ad caught my eye the other day.

Dairy Queen for Sale - Western Wisconsin
$60,000 ¼ down pymt. 715-123-4567

Hmmmm ... $60,000 and ¼ down is $15,000 ... that's pretty good. I didn't want one, but I called the guy out of curiosity. He told me he owned two stores in Western Wisconsin. He runs one and his wife runs the other. He drives an hour every morning to get to his store and an hour home every night. He said, "I'm tired of it and want to sell the store that I run."

He's open 8 months out of the year. I asked, "What's your store net?"

"About $30,000 a year," he said.

I inquired, "Okay, what do you take for a salary?"

"Nothing," He painfully conveyed.

I questioned "How much other help do you have?"

"Well *some* part-time high school help. But I'm here from 8 in the morning to 11 at night *every* day," he moaned.

I summed it up, "You're working for nothin'. You can get more *at a job* and work less!"

"I know," he confessed. "My kid works at Anderson Windows and makes $60,000 a year plus benefits."

Feeling a bit downhearted about his situation, I tried to bring some positive light to our conversation, "Well, I'll tell you one thing, this is the first Dairy Queen franchise I've ever seen where the price is reasonable, $60,000 and you only want $15,000 down?"

"NO! NO! NO!" he shouted. "You misread the ad! The price of the store is $240,000. The $60,000 is the ¼ down payment."

Now who would pay a quarter of a million dollars to work their fanny off for 8 months out of the year? You'd have to go *eight years* without any salary! The $30,000 each year would have to go to paying the $240,000 purchase price back.

This Dairy Queen owner is a good prospect! I've already sent a video to him. Franchise people and small business owners are some of your best prospects. They can *appreciate* the small investment in Nutrition For Life with the potential for a large return in comparison to what they have put into their current or past businesses.

Success Secret ...

"Ask business owners this question: 'Would you be interested in increasing your revenue with no extra overhead with the possibility of earning franchise income without franchise investment?'"

PART 11

Secrets Of
Highly Effective
Network Marketers

At our opportunity meetings I sometimes hold a contest with a $20 bill in my hand. I give the audience three minutes to write down names of people they know on a first name basis who are not in Nutrition For Life. You ought to watch them get writing. I had one person who thought of 72 people in 3 minutes. The purpose of this is more than awarding $20; each and every person in that room thought of new prospects and has a healthy new prospect list started. I've been in this company since 1985, and I still think of new names every day.

To increase the size of your prospect list, spend a couple hours monthly going through the Yellow Pages looking at every heading. Ask yourself, "Who do I know who is a _____." And fill in the blank with the heading from the Yellow Pages. Add these names to your list of prospects.

Every week I go through each state in the road atlas asking myself, "Who might I know?" I have a good memory, but I still think of new names. I'm always prospecting.

You probably receive letters from people in different programs. Save the senders' contact information because they are good future prospects. Right now is not the time to contact them back because they are mailing to you on what is usually their "hot" program — it still excites them.

Take all the solicitations you receive, and put them in a shoe box. Age those prospects for six months before you call them. After six months call them back. Seven out of ten will no longer be in their programs or will be unhappy with them, and they may take a look at your opportunity.

You want a good prospect list? Start clipping the network marketing classified ads from newspapers and shoppers. Place the ads in an envelope with the current date on it and put the envelope in a box for six months. Do this process weekly and in six months, you'll have new leads to call.

Six months is time enough to let the dream fall apart for many distributors with their current opportunity.

We all have the distributor in our organization who says, "I just don't know anybody. Golly, I don't know a soul."

I say, "Gosh, you're in a heck of a fix. You mean, if you died today, there would be no one at your funeral?"

"Oh, some folks would be at my funeral."

There you go, get pen and paper ready to write down

the list of the people who you think would attend your funeral. That's an old prospecting secret that's been working for years.

Here is a great tip for local sponsoring. When I have a prospect who is interested, I give out an audio sponsoring tape. There are many good sponsoring tapes to choose from in the Distributor Services catalogs.

When I hand my prospect the audio tape, I *don't* give them *details*. I let the tape do the work by putting it into their hands, looking into their eyes and saying, "This is a *hot* message! I'm excited about it ... but I don't want to sway your thinking. I want to know what you and your spouse think about it."

If my prospect is going to be climbing into his or her car to leave, I add, "Please ... if you're going to listen to this tape when you get in your car, do me a favor. Please, put the cruise control on because I don't want you to get a speeding ticket."

It happened to me in 1983! I became so excited, I pressed too hard on the gas and the red lights in the rear view mirror followed.

Sounds corny? It may be, but if I had a sign saying, "Wet Paint," people would walk over and touch the paint: "Oh, yeah, it's still wet." You have to build the same curiosity with the tape. I give out no paperwork or brochures with the tape. I don't want to overwhelm them and cause them not to listen to the tape.

When you hand your prospect the tape, tell him or her you're going to follow-up with a call in 24-hours. Friend, your best follow-up is in *24-hours*. You can't let them sit. My prospects have to *agree* that if I <u>loan</u> them a tape, they will listen to it *within* 24-hours. This is S.O.U. — Sense Of Urgency!

Don't ask them to call you — they won't. <u>You call them.</u> Tell them, "I will call you on (whatever day is 24-hours from your conversation). What's a good time? 7 p.m. or 8 p.m.?"

Agree on the time, then in a polite, business-like manner confirm the appointment by saying, "You are good at keeping appointments, aren't you?"

When I place the follow-up call, I don't ask, "How did you like the tape?" Most often, prospects will attempt to pull the wool over your eyes.

Instead, I ask, "Wasn't that tape fantastic?" This engages them into thinking about the tape. If they haven't listened to it yet, you will know immediately.

If they haven't listened to it and they are local say, "I'm coming over right now to pick it up." They usually reply, "No! No! No!" and I'll give them one more day — another 24-hours.

If they haven't listened to the tape in *two* days then you *haven't* got yourself a good prospect. If on the second day they haven't listened to it say, "I'll be out to pick it up. In 30 minutes I'll be at your place."

They will usually say, "No! No! No!" That's when you need to say, "I'll be over in 30 minutes" and hang up the phone and get in your car. There is a reason for this. What do you suppose they are doing as you are driving over? Eight out of ten will be watching the video or listening to the audio tape

— it's called "fear-of-loss." When you reach your prospect's home you'll probably have a one-on-one meeting.

One day a guy told me he was so worried I'd arrive at his home too quickly, he listened to the tape on fast forward. That's called major "fear-of-loss."

How do you get your new enrollees started? For those who start their businesses as executives, invest some of your $100 to $150 commission back into your distributor. I give my new executives 15 cassettes or 5 videos. What's in it for you?

Nutrition For Life's compensation plan is built on sponsoring and strengthening personal enrollees. How are your distributors going to become strong? You arm them with sponsoring ammunition.

Every time a personally enrolled executive sends you a copy of an application for a new executive, reload your enrollee with tools. To succeed, you must treat your Nutrition For Life opportunity as a business and re-invest some time and money back into your people.

Can you image what will happen to your business when you implement the investment principle? When you enroll a new *executive* — which is the level a person who wants to build the business selects — you give them 15 audio tapes or 5 video tapes. When *your* personal executive enrolls another executive *you* give *your* enrollee another 15 audios or 5 videos. In the meantime, your personal enrollee will give 15 audios or 5 videos to *their* personal enrollees who will give 15/5 to *their* personal enrollees. Your business will explode.

I've watched organizations increase by 100% to 200% a month once the sponsoring tools are being used by the downline in the field.

Once the tools are in the hands of distributors in your organization, they must get them into the hands of prospects. Dean Zaudtke of Minneapolis tries to put an audio cassette into ten prospects' hands everyday. This man is busy with his successful homebuilding business — last year he built over 100 homes — but he doesn't quit for the night until he has tried to put 10 cassettes out for the day.

You *want* busy people. When they say, "I'm too busy," you respond, "Great, that's just the type of person who succeeds in Nutrition For Life. Have you got 4 hours a week? I'll match it with 4 hours a week and that means every week you have 8 hours working for you. We'll sponsor someone and ask them for four hours a week. Don't be surprised if we have 100 hours a week working for you within 90 days."

When people tell you they are *too* busy it usually means *they don't have enough money*. If they want time freedom and money, Nutrition For Life is the business for them. Once busy people understand how their time can be duplicated in Nutrition For Life, they will be devoting more and more time to this business.

Success Secret ...

"Success is just a decision. The results will follow the work."

PART 12

Maloney on Marketing

Marketing is the engine that drives your business.

When advertising for network marketing opportunity meetings, daily local papers have worked the best for me in comparison to local "shoppers." "Shoppers" are the free papers loaded with classified ads which you find on newsstands around town. If a town does not have a daily paper, then I prefer the weekly paper to a "shopper." But very importantly, save your money and don't expect advertising to bring out anybody to an opportunity meeting. Word-of-mouth is the only way to get people to opportunity meetings.

I conducted a test in Ashland, Wisconsin, where I advertised for a home-based business seminar. The 3 inch x 6 inch display ad ran in the local paper and in the local "shopper." I received 52 reservations of which 46 came out of the daily paper and six out of the shopper.

You might say, "Hey, Dayle, six people sounds great.

How could you be upset with six people?"

Let's take a look at the *quality* of the six people from the "shopper." None of them had a job and they were all poor — both financially and mentally which is the toughest condition in existence.

What kind of ad do you place in the daily or weekly paper? A classified ad. I stay out of the sales opportunity column because those people are looking for a J-O-B and lack entrepreneurial thinking. The first clue is when they want to know the hourly wage or salary being paid.

You will find entrepreneurs in the business opportunity section. *USA Today* is a great place to advertise. It's time Nutrition For Life distributors start advertising in the *USA Today* Friday edition in the business opportunity section. A four line classified usually brings in about 50 to 75 leads. *Success Magazine* and *Entrepreneur Magazine* have also been good for me.

A technique I use when I am advertising in the business opportunity section is called back-ending a free offer. Run an ad offering a free tape:

> Call for the FREE tape that has allowed thousands of people to double their income (phone number).

I've used this technique for years in the *USA Today*. I offered a free tape called "Secrets of MLM." Information about Nutrition For Life was included with the free tape. It's one of the best recruiting techniques you'll ever find in classified advertising.

Now, that you have the ad placed, what kind of voicemail greeting should you have? If you are looking for women entrepreneurs, have a female voice mail greeting. We've compared the results of having my male voice to Marisa Young's voice on the voicemail greeting. Marisa's female voice receives twice as many leads from the same ad in the same paper running to capture the attention of women. Whether you want to record a woman's or a man's voice depends on who your target market is and what kind of ad you have running.

Make sure you say in your voicemail message, "There is no obligation" and "we will send you free information you can read in the privacy of your own home." The purpose of voicemail is to have your prospects leave their names, addresses, phone numbers and best time to call so you can call them and then send a tape out.

Before we send out a tape, we always call the prospects to verify the addresses and obtain an idea of their interest, or if they are just collecting free information.

When you do your follow-up calls on the mailed tapes, when is the best time to make those calls? Between 6 p.m. and 9 p.m. on Sunday nights is good because it's when most people are home. Don't let that stop you from calling the other nights also.

What other ads work? Believe it or not, you can do a lot of good with a little teaser ad in the personal column. I use real small one-line or two-line classifieds — cheapees — and run my ads for 7 days straight to receive a better price than running just one day.

I run curiosity ads in the personal columns with catchy headlines above the teaser copy. One that works for me is, "If this is yesterday's paper ... you may be too late." My gosh! They stop to look at the date to make sure they are holding today's paper. Then they go back and read.

I like to run ads in the lost and found section. My ad reads, "Found! The best part-time income opportunity in ..." (end the ad with the name of the community the ad is being placed in followed by your phone number).

I used to run a personal ad reading, "Who is Dayle?" (with my phone number). It drove them crazy in the small towns. They want to know, "My gosh! Who is that guy? He's still in the paper." They actually called me to find out. Remember, the purpose of the ad is to make the telephone ring.

An insurance man in Idaho, Sam Hunt, ran that ad everywhere. He also had bumper stickers saying, "Who is Sam Hunt?" with his phone number. He became a legend in his area.

Several years ago in a small Idaho town, during the annual Labor Day Parade, Sam Hunt was the Grand Marshall. On both sides of the convertible it read, "*This* is Sam Hunt!" All the folks were excited to finally find out who Sam Hunt was. It was driving them crazy.

I saw an ad the other day in Orange County, California, and called but couldn't get through — it was busy all the time. The ad read, "Divorce Sale. His stuff cheap! (phone number).

A little tip on your ads: if you're going to have a recorded message phone number, also show a live number — people are tired of just hearing recorded messages. Some people like the no-obligation recording but others want to talk to you right now. You'll receive 20 calls in the voicemail box to one live call. The one live call is the person who's going to become Platinum — a real leader in your organization.

One of my favorite topics is business cards. Put your picture on your company business card. Prospects will keep your card forever if it has your picture on it. When was the last time you went through the family photo album or photo drawer and threw away pictures? I still have a realtor's business card from years ago. Why do you suppose I kept his card? It has his picture on it.

You'll be mailing out tapes to people you've never met face-to-face. If you have the picture on your card, when you do the phone follow-up, they feel like they've known you for years — you're part of the family. They'd say to me, "Dayle, you look like Grandpa Ben," or "You remind me of Uncle Jack."

Fantastic! This is a relationship business, and because of my picture on my business card, they feel like they already know me.

Friend, if you read this book and do nothing else but put your picture on your card — you're probably going to double your sponsoring results.

You've got to promise to use a current picture. If you're 40-years-old, don't you dare use a high school graduation picture. To keep costs low, you can put a black and white picture on your card.

I don't like the real expensive business cards. You know why? You buy yourself expensive business cards, and you'll become a collector of your own cards: "Well, I wonder if I should give them one? They're 28 cents. No, I don't think

I will."

Business cards will never increase in value like baseball cards. They only become an asset when you hand them out. I leave my cards everywhere.

I like to have a little saying on my business card that just forces them to call me. Here's the saying I've used for years, and it has always worked: "If you continue to think like you've always thought, you'll continue to get what you've always got. Is it enough?" If not, write or call (your contact information goes here).

It drives people crazy. I've been using it for years, and some folks think I was the originator of that saying but I wasn't. I found it written in pencil on a men's restroom wall in The Big Texas Truck Stop in Amarillo, Texas.

Another technique I've used with good results is a 1" x 1" business card. They cost about $10 per 1000. I give them out everywhere to everybody. I don't just give people one, I give them a handful. The reason these cards work is the saying on the backside, "If I had some of your business, I could afford a larger card." They work because it gets them to laugh and they remember you for it. In network marketing you have to build relationships and it helps to be memorable.

Now, if you're ever without a business card, take out your checkbook and write a personal check for *$1.00*. Fill in their name and write one dollar. Hand it over and say, "Here's a business card you can keep." I've never had anybody cash a $1.00 check They'll hang on to it forever and remember you for it.

On my business cards, I used to put initials after my name. It's an easy way to break the ice because it opens people up and gets the conversation started.

Some initials I've used after my name are: A. F.

People ask, "What's AF stand for?"

I say, "Almost Famous."

M.E.E has been good. It stands for Master of Economic Enjoyment.

P.H.D. stands for Past Having Debts or Past Having Doubts or Poor Hungry and Driven.

P.H.D.D means Doctor of Dollars. M.B.A is Mega Bank Account.

Then my old stand-by for years — Dayle Maloney, D.M.N. They'd always say to me, "What's the DMN. stand for?"

I'd laugh, "It Don't Mean Nothing." Those little ice breakers will help you start conversations — which is the basis for building your business and the relationship.

Make sure when you send out your tapes that the envelopes are hand addressed or typed directly on to the envelope — no labels. Computer labels smell of the junk mail. Also, use a postage stamp, never metered mail. It looks too much like a mass mailing — which is considered junk mail and thrown away before it is opened.

Want to have your prospect open your envelope? Mail the envelope with 32-1¢ stamps on it. Why? It looks important and it's going to get opened up. All you're trying to do is get your envelope opened. It's a good job for your kids and involves them in the family business.

Do you have any people in your organization who are inactive? Folks who you've sponsored, then who leave you wondering if they've left the state — are they dead or alive? You can't get ahold of them because their phone has been disconnected or it's unlisted. They don't call you or come to functions and they don't buy product.

There is a way to get in touch with them, if they are still around. This is what we used to do with inactive people. We hand address an envelope to them and put our phone number as part of the return address. Then we seal the envelope and <u>send</u> it <u>out</u> <u>empty</u>. Try it. Send inactive people an empty envelope. Make sure your <u>name</u> and <u>phone</u> <u>number</u> are on the return address.

Almost everyone will call you when they receive it and say, "I got this envelope and there's nothing in it."

"What is supposed to be in there is a letter about the next meeting," you kindly inform them with excitement in your voice. You're going to find out if there is any hope for this person or if it is best to cut the rope and move on. You can't hang with those people forever. It's usually easier to give birth to a new enrollee than it is to resurrect a dead one.

The next time you are sending out tapes with a cover letter, I want you to try this. It's a little crazy, but I do it myself and it works. Crumple the cover letters — just like you were going to throw them away. Keep each letter in one piece — don't tear it. Then straighten the letter back out but don't unwrinkle it too much. Before you put it in the envelope use a blue felt pen and write across the top of each letter ... "Please, do not throw this away again."

Now, put the crumpled letter in the envelope and send it out. Wrinkling the letter is another good job for the kids to be involved in the family business.

I recommended this to a college graduate who couldn't find a job in his field for 14 months. He had sent out all kinds of resumes. Using the wrinkle secret he secured a job in his field in 10 days. A commercial bill collector — who was paid for collecting delinquent accounts — wrinkled up a copy of each overdue bill and sent them to the debtors. It worked well for him.

Success Secret ...

> "People who don't advertise are
> like people who wink in the dark ...
> they know what they're doing but
> nobody else does."

PART 13

How To Interest Realtors and Entrepreneurs in Network Marketing

Let me tell you how we sponsor realtors and successful entrepreneurs into this business. We don't ask those business people to come to the evening meetings. We have business luncheons at the country club and buy their lunch. We never have more than 15 people at the luncheon.

Dale Brunner was in charge of a luncheon. He invited seven realtors in addition to the two of us. We had a little room at the country club with tables and chairs for the 9 people and an area for the speaker up front. At 12:00 sharp the food was served, and by 1 p.m. the meeting was over.

We didn't give details about how the compensation plan worked; that wasn't the purpose of the business luncheon. The purpose was to convince our guests that long-term residual income was something they needed to consider. The goal was by the time the luncheon was over our guests would agree to take the video or audio home and view it or listen to it that evening.

We didn't give out product catalogs, just the video or cassette tape. Any other details and questions would be answered in the follow-up.

Our results? We sponsored three out of the seven

realtors as Executives in Nutrition for Life at the $699 level.

You see, once we have enrolled someone through the luncheon, he or she can bring guests to the next luncheon. We like to do one luncheon every week.

We work for a month with the people we sponsor through the luncheons before we have them attend the regular meetings on Tuesday nights.

We invite prospects to the luncheons or our office. If we are going to have prospects come to an evening meeting at a hotel, we'll meet them for dinner <u>before</u> <u>the</u> <u>meeting</u>.

Every week people say to me, "Oh,, I'm so excited! I've got a big-time network marketer coming to the meeting tonight." My distributor will be in the hotel looking for the guest who doesn't show. Those 'big fish' normally are not going to show, friend. You have to work those people eyeball-to-eyeball and get them sponsored before they will start showing up at meetings.

Success Secret ...

"When you talk to a successful business person, present this opportunity by first answering the question which is naturally on everyone's minds: 'What's in it for me?'"

PART 14

Five Hot Facts
and One-Liners

I follow the Nutrition For Life system when presenting the opportunity, but here are a few things I try to mention during an opportunity meeting.

This is a fun business. You work from your home. It's a proven fact that 78% of employed people hate their jobs. Do you know what corporate America's nightmare is today? Dying of a heart attack at the desk. I can't find anybody who hates their "job" in Nutrition For Life. In a recent business magazine survey, white-collar professionals were asked if they would take a 20% pay cut to have 20% more time with their families. Ninety-six percent said, "Yes."

In this business you can't get fired or laid off! I have between 40,000 and 50,000 distributors in my downline. I also have 9 people working for me in Eau Claire. It seems like quite often there are one or more of my nine employees who call in sick or can't make it to the office. Out of 50,000 distributors, I have yet to have the first distributor call in sick.

In the opportunity meeting, I remind the audience that the network marketing industry has existed for decades and Nutrition For Life has been in business since 1984. You only have a future if the company has a future.

When I show the plan whether it is one-on-one or at an opportunity meeting, I use 3rd party testimonials and drop names throughout the presentation. This is a people business. People want to know that other people are succeeding.

Success Secret ...

"Use Nutrition For Life's proven system-of-success for presenting the opportunity and sprinkle your presentation with problems which Nutrition For Life solves."

PART 15

Doctors Speak Out On Network Marketing

Drs. Tom and Ann Klesmit,
5-Star Platinum Executives, Texas
Network Marketing: The Most Ingenious And Credible
Business Decision A Person Could Ever Make

The first time Dr. Ann and I ever saw Dayle Maloney we said to ourselves, "If this gentleman can produce the income that we are talking about then we think anyone can."

When I first investigated the company before we became involved, I had my attorney and my financial consultant take a look. Because Dayle was the highest money earner, I also had them check him out. My first impression of Dayle was when my consultants verified the amount of money he was making and the size of his organization. They discovered he was actually earning that which he claimed, anywhere from between $120,000 to $170,000 a month. He had been in Nutrition For Life for 11 years at that time and his influence was very pervasive through out the industry, known as "Mr. Network Marketing." This information was important to me because when I looked at the opportunity, if it couldn't earn me $100,000 a month, I wasn't interested. Dayle was one of the big earners in Nutrition For Life, and I based my standards on him.

Dayle has taught me that to succeed in network marketing, you have to get down to the grassroots level; that is the most important thing I have learned. The vast majority of people are looking to make an extra $300 to $400 a month. If you don't relate to people who are on that level, your organization will never grow.

A great feature of our company is we have about 400 different products for people to build their businesses on. When we consider there are 18 million people in the U.S. alone who suffer from rheumatoid arthritis, Nutrition For Life's Artho-Support Tri-Pak, in my mind, comes as close to helping arthritis as you can.

I would also say the St. John's Wort is a tremendous product which can possibly be a replacement for Prozac. Prozac has multiple, multiple, multiple side effects and most people can immediately understand why St. John's Wort is so important. When you can recommend St. John's Wort, and it will relieve many depression symptoms naturally, you have a tremendous product.

You have to elevate your belief to a level of credibility with other people before you can build the business. If you don't believe in what you are doing, you are never going to be successful and this applies to anything in life. I ask patients every day about their jobs. Not only do they not like their jobs, they really don't believe there is a benefit in doing them.

Let's understand why network marketing is such a tremendous opportunity and why Nutrition for Life is the number one company in this industry. If people can believe, then all the techniques they learn — like how to contact people and handle objections — those almost become irrelevant. When you believe, you start talking to people from your heart, and it is amazing how people will join the business.

Here is what I find very intriguing about network marketing. People say network marketing provides financial *freedom*, and I'd have to agree with them 100%. Whether you see it as an investment or a business opportunity, it is the only opportunity I see right now which provides financial *security*.

What is the difference? Look at traditional businesses, stocks and bonds, franchises, real estate, and any other opportunity where someone can earn money. There are two principles lacking. Network marketing is the only option for people where they can have no principle in a savings account and yet collect an interest check. It allows people to make money from sharing in the abilities of other people.

Traditionally, we have been taught to save money, and some day we will get an interest check. A study conducted several months ago concluded the average American starts saving money at age 35 and, finally, by age 57, accumulates $100,000. That is not liquid money; it is their home equity, pension plan, IRA, savings, and checking.

Take the $100,000 and divide it by 12 months; then multiply it by 5%. What you would find is the average American would receive an interest check of $500 per month. Is that good? Well, it takes the average American 22 years to get a $500 interest check. The study reveals from age 57 to 73 — another 16 years — that the $100,000 could compound to $600,000 if the interest is left in the account. Divide $600,000 by 12 and multiply it by 5%, and a person has a $3000 per month interest check. The average person in America needs 38 years to accumulate a residual income of $36,000 a year.

I would hope I could say it gets better, but it doesn't because out of 100 people who are 65 years of age, 34 of them are dead. If we are talking 73 year olds, most people aren't even going to reap the benefit.

Well, let's talk about Dayle Maloney, Kevin Trudeau, Tom Klesmit and a whole bunch of individuals in network marketing. Within three months, if I had quit building my network marketing business, I would have had a check of $500 a month for the rest of my life. In comparison, it takes the average American 22 years to do what took me three months. How about the average guy who is doing the business at an average pace? What if it took him two years...compared to 22 years?

I think network marketing is the most ingenious business decision a person could ever make. There are people building their Nutrition For Life business who are in their sixth month and ninth month and already earning $3000 per month residual income. It takes the average American 38 years to do the same without network marketing.

What if it took a person 5 years to make $5000 a month in residual income? It still would be the most brilliant business decision they ever made. This is the only opportunity on the planet which doesn't require much principle and that makes network marketing intriguing.

This is also the only opportunity which offers shared diversification, meaning sharing a risk. When a person joins your organization they will produce income for you every month. When another person joins, it happens again.

Right now, as a doctor, if I don't go to work, I don't get paid. If a person was to become ill, do they get paid? Well, maybe for a couple weeks, but then they are on their own. If they want to retire — because of Nutrition For Life, I just retired at age 43 — where is the income going to come from? Most of us in life produce the income. If we don't produce it, we don't take it home. Network marketing shares the abilities of other people to produce income for you.

Most white collar people have to work 60 to 80 hours per week to create the income in order to maintain their lifestyle. All of a sudden, they realize for the first time in their lives, *someone else* can produce income for them — this is very intriguing. When they want to go on vacation, if they get sick, when they want to retire — people are making money when they are not working and it is unbelievably nice. In my opinion, this is why over the next 5 years *everyone* will be flocking to network marketing. Economists predict 80% of the American population will own a home-based business by the year 2005 and I agree, there will be no option.

Network marketing is a avenue for people who normally would not be able to change their lives. Statistically, we know if the average American were able to make an additional $300 per month, it would completely change their life. It means an extra $300 would pay the Sears, Penney's, and Wards charge cards down quicker, or the family could go to Disneyland — when they couldn't before. With our program, they would have the potential for a free car and this would take that debt off their back.

How else could the average person do this? Most forms of creating residual income require money. If you want to earn money from stocks, real estate, or a franchise, you would first need money to invest. Network marketing is the only way I know which allows people with a very small investment to produce sizable residual income which will change a vast majority of lives around the world.

**Drs. Tom and Ann Klesmit have three children:
Destiny, Brandon, and Jordan**

Success Secret ...

> "Gather the facts, make your decision,
> take action now."

PART 16

Sponsoring Made Easy

Jim & Jo Horn,
4-Star Platinum Executives, California
How To Find Those People Who Want To
Build A Network Marketing Business

Five years ago the woman I was dating at the time —
who became my wife, Jo — was involved in a network
marketing company. She dragged me to meetings. I was a
retired jet fighter pilot and was currently earning a nice living
as a stock broker. If it weren't for Jo, I don't think I would
have ever taken a serious look at network marketing.

The company we were involved with at the time went
out of business. I didn't like what we experienced and decided
to leave the network marketing industry. I really wanted
nothing more to do with it.

A friend from my previous company, Tracy Dieterich,
had been to one of Dayle Maloney's generic MLM seminars a
couple years before. Dayle kept in touch with his seminar

attendees. At some point during the late fall of 1995, Tracy received a mailing from Dayle and called me to say, "We should look seriously at this."

I knew Dayle was a giant in the industry. He was known in all network marketing circles as a tremendous teacher and someone who really worked closely with people — the type of mentoring we did not have in our last company.

Tracy and I decided we would join Dayle's organization. We immediately flew to a rally in Minneapolis, Minnesota, and into a terrible snow storm. We figured nobody would show up, but to our amazement, there were almost *5,000 people* at this rally, frothing at-the-mouth. At that moment, we knew we had made the right choice.

I've been fortunate to be mentored by Dayle Maloney who is one of the most loveable and unassuming people I've ever known. He would rather give and bend than force his own way. I've spent enough time to know that's genuinely Dayle; it's not a put on. He's taught me more about the industry, life and how to deal with people than I can ever explain. I watch what Dayle does and try to imitate it as best I can.

I spent three weeks with him in Canada doing seminars, and by the third week my tongue was dragging. Dayle was just pumping right along, and I was having a hard time getting that enthusiastic up-feeling for each seminar.

Here's one of his secrets (I don't even know if he realizes this happens): something magical occurs when Dayle puts his tie on, which he doesn't like to do, by the way. He can be totally exhausted, but when that tie goes on he becomes energized. It's like baseball players putting on their jerseys or artists picking up their brushes.

Being on the road with Dayle and trying to keep up with him exhausts me. I'm several years younger than Dayle and in better health, but he outworks me. How does he do that?

After the tour was all done, we were both ready to relax. I had learned there was no way I was going to outwork this guy.

I don't think people realize how tired Dayle is when he goes from city-to-city or how tough he feels sometimes. He can be experiencing excruciating pain, exhaustion, headaches or just plain not feeling well, but he keeps on going. Dayle really wants to give *every single person* the best he can and be right there with them. He inspires people — lets them know they can do anything they believe they can. He says, "Even if only one person shows up, they deserve the *best* presentation I can possibly give them."

Dayle is the defender of the dream. He helps people start dreaming again, holding on to their dreams and believing they can achieve them. That's important work in the midst of a world full of dream stealers and we've all seen our share of dream stealers.

Who is the number one dream stealer most people have? Their spouses. The spouse usually doesn't come out and say, "I forbid you from doing this business." Instead they indirectly steal the dream by their lack of support or when they make fun of going to meetings or going to trainings. It's not like the dream stealer spouse withholds anything — but uneasy feelings are multiplied because it's our spouse. We all want our husband or wife's approval.

I attended an opportunity meeting and there was a guy

I knew. I said, "Joe (we'll change the name to protect the innocent), I didn't know you were in this business."

He said, "I'm not in this business. This is Nancy's business. I just came along to keep her company tonight."

I had known Joe and Nancy for a while. Nancy was and still is a bundle of energy.

Joe sat through the meeting rather uninterested. Meantime, Nancy had been building a great business. Her checks were over $1,000 a month on a part-time basis.

Joe came back to another meeting about 3 month later. I said, "Joe, how's the business coming?"

He said, "*We're* doing real good!" It's so typical.

When people in your organization are dealing with dream stealers, you have to become the support system for the person whose dream is being jeopardized. If I see people who could really build their businesses and they want to, but their spouse is not supportive, I will become the support system for them.

These are people I will call more frequently. I will spend more time recognizing the positive things going on in their businesses. Maybe we'll do lunch or more appointments together. I try to overcome the damage the dream stealer is doing. Dayle does that a lot, too.

Success in our industry is achieved by increasing a person's belief level to the point where they don't care if they talk to people who don't have the same level of belief — whether it be friends, a spouse or whomever.

The biggest reason your new enrollees don't sponsor new people into this business is fear of rejection by their friends and family. Your new person's belief level has to be high enough to where they can overcome it. Of course, going to events can help. The most important step is to help your new enrollee start an organization and earn bonus checks. In Nutrition For Life, they can also earn a free car.

I can increase my new enrollee's belief level simply by being there, being positive and helping them build the business. It can be tedious work and you will have to commit to yourself to stick with it. When you accept the responsibility of sponsoring someone, then you have a commitment to stick with them and help them succeed.

How many people who you sponsor will really put forth the effort to build their own business? I've sponsored 74 people into this business and 8 have achieved Platinum at one time or another. Now, there are others growing their businesses, just not at the same feverish rate as those 8 who've achieved Platinum. Those people who grow their businesses with one or two enrollees every now and again or don't build at all, require less time from me because they are not as active.

So the real question: "How many people must you sponsor to find those 4 or 5 to work with?"

That number might be 10, 20 or 100 because it is a function of how you go about prospecting and sponsoring. I've discovered survey results which show 7% of the American population has an interest in looking at a part-time business opportunity in network marketing. These are the business builders.

The survey also revealed 44% of the people

interviewed had an interest in purchasing products from a network marketing company. These are the preferred customers who want to join Nutrition For Life to be able to purchase products at wholesale but are probably not going to build a business.

To grow our organizations solidly and quickly, *sort* through people looking for the 7% who *want* a network marketing business. What most of us do is attempt to convince everyone on the planet they *need* to join our business. People take action based on what they *want* to do, not what they *need* to do. How efficiently we sort through prospects and find the magic 7% is going to determine in how many people we will need to sponsor to find the business builders.

Just knowing you are looking for the 7% of the American population who are looking for a part-time business opportunity will help you a great deal. The "sorting" versus "convincing" system-of-success is at the heart of our prospecting challenge.

As a sponsor or upline, I help people learn how to "sort" versus "convince". How? Ask the *right questions* of your prospect to discover if they have an interest. You are looking for people who want to make a change in their lives, not those who are happy being in whatever rut they exist.

Unfortunately, most people are not *uncomfortable* enough to want to make a change. Making a change means they will have to get out of their comfort zone.

How do I determine if a prospect is ready? I ask them one of two questions: "Are you making all the money you'd like to make?" -or- "Would you like to earn some extra money?"

I think there are three reasons people start a network marketing business: money, time or control. More-money is the motivation about 60% of the time. Money will also be involved in the more-time and more-control-over-their-life desires of which both may mean a career shift or increase in the amount of money your prospect takes home each month.

In those two cases, money is going to be *involved* but may not be *the prime motivator*. When you are talking to a high-powered executive with a six-figure income and ask, "Do you want to make some extra money?" That really isn't going to be the motivation or hot button. This is a person who may want more time or control over his or her life.

First, discover if the person you're talking to is going to be motivated to make a life change by any of those three reasons: more-money, more-time, more-control. How do you uncover their motive?

When I meet people I ask, "What do you do for a living?" I try to put a positive spin on my reply. How? Whatever they do for a living I say, "Oh, that must be very interesting. You must get all kinds of job satisfaction and make all the money you want to make?"

Most often people say, "Are you crazy? I'm working my tail off and make nowhere near enough money!"

Then I will LISTEN and let them tell me what it is that they want out of life.

To make a point, turn this conversation around and we'll ask someone, "What do you do for a living?"

They say, "I am an architect."

We reply, "How can you stand to do that?"

What is the probable reply we will receive? The person will become very defensive and will justify all the reasons why she or he is an architect.

Ask people about their lives using the questions I've given you. Those questions will efficiently assist you in sorting through the masses of people to identify those whose answers tell you they want to make a change in their lives.

People eventually ask, "Well, what do you do?"

I share with them what I do and *why*. My reason is directly linked to what my prospect wants — which is usually more money, more time, or more control. Determine in advance three answers to why you have chosen this business for each situation.

When you meet the prospect and discover they want more time, tell them why you choose Nutrition For Life to enjoy more time and what you've done or will do with your additional time. They want more money? Tell them why you started your Nutrition For Life business to earn more money and some of what you do or will do with your money. They want more control over their lives? Share with them why you wanted the same and what you can do now that you have achieved it or what you will do once you achieve it.

If I can peak some level of interest in a prospect, then I'll go to the next step which is an audio tape or video tape. Let the tape do the work for you.

In my organization, I've noticed, using the sorting technique, it leads to a challenge — which is wonderful to have: How many people can you really *work with* all at one time?

I've found the optimal number of people I can work with, who want to become leaders all at the same time, is four or five. I had seven people become Platinum leaders simultaneously in January of this year and, believe me, I had my hands full trying to keep up with them. It was a lot of work. They all made it, but that was too many at once.

In my 20 years as a Marine fighter pilot (including being one of the fighter pilots flying a jet in the Hollywood movie TOP GUN) and 8 years as a stock broker, there was nothing that prepared me for network marketing. In fact, quite the opposite. I was a very traditional, conservative businessman and there was no way I was ever going to look at "one of those things."

People need to be patient with folks they want to sponsor into the business. I turned down many different friends of mine through the years who wanted me to look at network marketing, and today it is my full-time career. There are numerous other people who have made a similar career switch. With those conservative, traditional business people who haven't made the switch to network marketing yet, be patient and keep in contact. Eventually they will take a look.

Jo & Jim Horn
4-Star Platinum Executives, California

Success Secret ...

"Seven percent of the American population has an interest in considering a part-time business opportunity in network marketing. Your mission is to find them."

Chapter 8

And Now For The Rest Of The Story...

PART 1

Some Things Don't Make Sense

People tell me they enjoy my talks. Thinking back to where I started, it just doesn't make sense. In high school, I was real shy, but I always knew the answer. I was just *too scared* to raise my hand. I took Speech 101 at the University of Minnesota. When the teacher announced I was to speak the next day, I couldn't go. I dropped the course.

I started selling recreational vehicles and did pretty well at it. Somehow, someone convinced me to give my first major speech at the National Recreational Vehicle Dealers Association annual meeting at Freedom Hall in Louisville, Kentucky. There were 8,000 people in the audience.

I was so nervous, I hadn't slept for two nights. It was terrible! I was sweating and pacing the floor.

About 10 minutes before I was to walk on stage, I thought, "I'd better put on my tie."

My hands were shaking, and I had used my handkerchief to mop the sweat off my brow. In the restroom mirror I struggled with the knot I had made when *a lady* said, "You're nervous aren't you, sir?"

That's a true story. My mind was so consumed with how scared I was that I had walked into the women's restroom.

There are a lot of things that just don't make sense. You've heard I fly all the time. At the airport, I'm always the last guy in the line when they call the flight because I don't walk very well. It never fails, and just the other day it happened again. I was in the back of the line and this guy came rushing up to me with his brief case. He was out of wind and he asked, "Is this the back of the line?"

"No, this is the front of the line. We're just all standing backwards," I replied with a friendly smile. It didn't make sense.

Women go to the beauty salon for permanents. I don't know why they don't call them *temporaries*. They go so often.

You go to a shoe store and you get a pair of shoes. Go buy a pair of pants and you only get *one*.

But the one that's always puzzled me — does anyone know why they have an expiration date on sour cream? What happens after the date?

For two weeks straight in the Eau Claire newspaper there was a quarter page ad for the Fifth Annual Eau Claire Psychic Conference. It read:

Attention All Psychics!
5th Annual Psychic Conference

My question was this — why are they running an ad? They should all know about it, shouldn't they?

Eau Claire now has its first full-time psychic reader. Last week there was a handwritten note on the front door. It read: "Closed today due to unforeseen circumstances."

If you throw a cat out of a car window does it become kitty litter?

When a cow laughs does milk come out its nose?

How do they get deer to cross at those yellow deer crossing signs?

Why do kamikaze pilots wear helmets?

What was the best thing *before* sliced bread?

Why do we park in a driveway and drive on a parkway?

I saw a commercial on TV last week. It said, "Illiterate? Write the President's Council on Literacy, Washington, D.C."

I saw a newspaper ad which read: "cured ham" — I wondered what the problem was.

I feel sorry for first-time flyers. They nervously arrive at the airport and the first thing they see is … terminal.

So often the airlines will load a wheel chair passenger on the plane first. As the plane is nearing its destination ,the flight attendant makes the major announcement: "Will the person who needs a wheelchair stay on the plane."

Why do they have interstate highways in Hawaii?

If corn oil comes from corn, where does baby oil come from?

Here is one of my classics: Why do noses run and feet smell?

Have you ever received a nasty letter or demand for payment with the words "final notice" stamped across the top? You wouldn't think you'd ever hear from them again, would you?

Here are more things that don't make sense.

When you open a new bag of cotton balls is the top one meant to be thrown away?

We have our first drive-through ATM machine in Eau Claire. It's also in Braille.

Why is a carrot more orange than an orange?

How do they get those "keep off the grass" signs where they are?

What do you do if you see an endangered animal eating an endangered plant?

Why don't sheep shrink when it rains?

If a multiple personality person threatens suicide is it a hostage situation?

If a parsley farmer is sued, can they garnish his wages?

Here is David Bertrand's favorite:

If a man speaks in the forest and there is no woman to hear him, is he still wrong?

Funeral processions have a police-escort through red lights. What's the hurry?

Why doesn't glue stick to the inside of the bottle?

Tell a man there are 400 billion stars and he'll believe you. Tell a man the bench has wet paint and he has to go find out.

If athletes get athlete's foot what do astronauts get? Mistletoe.

When you deal with investment advisors why are they called brokers and not richers?

You know what else doesn't make sense? You work at that same J-O-B for 30 years and you're no better off today, than when you started 30 years ago. Now that doesn't make sense to me.

I'm not knocking the job, but you have to give Nutrition For Life every spare minute.

Do you know what else doesn't make sense? More people have $250 cash in their pocket at age 18 than they do at age 68 ... after 50 years out there in the work force. Friends, that doesn't add up.

It makes sense to give this business everything it takes. Set your goals high. Aim a little higher, it doesn't hurt the gun. Aim for the sky . Don't aim for the barn because you may not clear the manure pile. You have to aim high! Aim for an eagle; bag a pheasant; just don't eat crow, that's all.

Success Secret ...

"You can't build a business on what you're going to do."

PART 2

You Could Be Just One Degree From Success

Some people reading this book are so close to total success, and they don't even realize it.

See, you've got to build a foundation and once it's built, you're ready to spread your wings and fly. Realize when you first start, you'll never know exactly what the success you will achieve is going to look like.

Here's how close you can be. Water will boil at 212 degrees Fahrenheit, but at 211 degrees it is just plain hot water. Understand that *one extra degree* gives that pot of hot water a whole head of steam. That's how close you may be to success.

To succeed, you must have "stickability" — the kind nothing can stop. I have people who say to me, "Well, I'm in the program and I'm going to see if it works before I do anything."

That's as stupid as anything I've ever heard anybody say — I'm in, but I'm going to *see* if it works. Why waste the energy even looking? You have to stay with it and work your business in order to see results. "Stickability" without personal activity on your part, is stupidity.

I've heard them say, "Well, I'm in...but I've shelved it over the summer."

Hey, you didn't put this company on the shelf! You put *yourself* on the shelf. This company is going to the top — with or without you. This train is moving on and you need to be on it. Get off the shelf and get back to work!

Success Secret ...

"The only place where success comes before work is in the dictionary."

PART 3

Success Is What You Make Of It

You've got to work with the people who *want* to build their business. You *can't force* anyone to succeed in this business.

For years, I've tried to keep people from quitting. I've practically built their businesses for them. Did it work? No. We can't pull people across the finish line. Find the people who *want* to do it and work with them. You can pull a rope, but you can't push it.

Here's a good rule of thumb: run with the runners; walk with the walkers; but just don't sit with the sitters.

Find the people who are at the point in their life where they *want* to <u>succeed</u>. Those are the people who you run like crazy with.

What does running with the runners mean? There are 5 very basic success principles that explain the thought process you and your runners need to agree on.

First is the *investment principle*. You and your team must invest time and some money in this business.

Second is the *association principle*. You and your group have to associate with successful people — people who want to or are taking action to achieve what you want to accomplish. It makes sense. You want a cold? Hang around with folks who have a cold — you're going to get a cold. Associate with people who have achieved what you want and you'll join their ranks.

Next is the *dream setting and getting principle*. You and your team must have dreams and set goals — both individual and as a team. Write them down on an unlined sheet of white paper with blue ink. That's a powerful Kevin Trudeau technique — it works! Get those dreams written down!

Forth is the *skills and techniques principle*. It's one thing to associate with the people who have what you want; it's totally different to have them train you. Training usually costs big money. Most people think when they pay $50,000 and more to a college that they have been trained for a lifetime. Not so. College only prepares you for more training.

To be guaranteed to excel in life, you need to invest in ongoing training. I know successful people who spend hundreds of dollars a month — learning. Become a continual student who takes action on what you have learned. Few colleges offer entrepreneur courses. Of those that do, many of them are taught by people who have never known what it's like to own their own businesses. Subscribe to the Master Developer Series forever — I don't think you can build a business without it.

Please, please, please ... if you remember nothing else, remember this: If you want to know how to do something, learn from someone who has already accomplished it successfully.

How popular is network marketing? It has existed for decades but in the last 10 years, the baby-boomers have latched on to it and won't let go. The casual, yet successful work atmosphere people can enjoy from home is becoming increasingly desired — everyone wants it.

Fifth is the *delayed gratification principle*. I could have easily quit when I received my first network marketing check for $5.66 — remember that was $7,000,000.00 ago. Instead, I realized I was working for delayed gratification. I knew in the beginning I'd do a lot I wouldn't get paid for, but later I would get paid for a lot I didn't do.

Success Secret ...

"To achieve success you must be willing to believe successful results to be true without seeing them first. Winners have a total belief before the results ever start happening."

PART 4

The Crazy Way
I Succeeded in
Network Marketing

Tom "Big Al" Schreiter,
Co-Founder of Nutrition For Life
This Opportunity Is What You Make Of It

Author's Note: Tom "Big Al" Schreiter is the world famous author of the "Big Al" recruiting books. More than 10,000,000 copies of the "Big Al" books have been sold to network marketing distributors worldwide.

As a 23-year old husband and father-to-be, I had a choice between one of two options to earn more money: a part-time job or a part-time business. The part-time business sounded better than working another job.

Back then network marketing was different. First of all, nobody knew how to do it. There were no books, tapes or seminars. Therefore, we all did it poorly.

At that time it was hard to get somebody sponsored because they thought you were a Communist or an anti-government hippie. Once you sponsored a person, they stayed in. Today it's different. It's easy to sponsor people, but by that afternoon they are in three other programs.

I started off my network marketing career with one year and ten months of absolute failure. I had no distributors and no retail customers. After 22 months of trying, something clicked and the last 23 years have been pretty awesome. What I mean is I have time and money freedom. I watched my kids grow up and I participated in their lives ... you know, annoyed them year round.

How do most people try to succeed in network marketing? They search for a company to make them rich. They consider success to be outside of themselves. Therefore, they have to find the perfect company at the perfect time where it will be 100% right with all the right products etc. etc. etc.

That's not possible. All companies have problems because they hire humans. When humans come on board, perfection goes downhill. What people don't realize is that success has nothing to do with the company. It has everything to do with the distributors themselves.

What they are doing is looking outside themselves for a "perfect" situation: a company going into momentum or a company just starting off. The fact is people join *you* ... not the company. The most important resource to develop is yourself so you attract people. People are always looking for leaders who know what they're doing.

How does a person become an MLM magnet? By learning and living the basic principles of human nature and public relations. Why would anyone want to learn new skills? Other people want the information and skills you have. They are attracted to you when you have what they want.

Here's an example. Let's say you are a guest at a party. If you have information on how to build a part-time business in sales and marketing, and people want that information, there will be a crowd around you.

You're at the same party but complaining about your last operation, that your dog ran away and your children don't love you ... chances are you're speaking to a vacuum. You don't have the information people want.

When you are making your selection between companies, do you judge an opportunity based on product, compensation, or management and founders? The answer is management and founders.

You really wouldn't want to join only on compensation because the management can always change the plan. You don't want to join based on products only because the company can add products and delete products. The company can improve products or make them worse.

So you are back to the management of the company. What is in their hearts? What is in the owner's heart? If they are looking for a quick payday, the first time the company shows red ink, they close the doors. If this company is their life-long vision, they're going to see it through no matter what happens.

My next statement might be rather shocking to some people so be prepared: Nutrition For Life is not going to make you rich, famous, or successful. What the heck am I talking about? Only *you* are going to make yourself rich, famous, or successful. But you can be confident that Nutrition For Life will hold up its end of the deal.

I've known Dayle when he was rich, and I've known Dayle when he was poor, and I still don't see any difference. Over the course of the 13 years Dayle and I have known each other, I've heard people say, "Dayle doesn't have a clue. He just doesn't get it. He loans money to people who never, ever pay him back. He's taken advantage of by people. He spends a lot of time helping people from whom he'll never, ever see a paycheck. Dayle just doesn't get it."

Now the funny thing is, Dayle makes a million or two a year. Hmmm ... I would have to say that those people — *just don't get it!*

Tom and Sue Schreiter with Dayle and Jeannine Maloney

Success Secret ...

"There are only three ways to make more money: through individual effort, with money, or by motivating people. Only one is limitless."

PART 5

Dayle Maloney's First Distributor

Pat Johnson, Gold Executive, Washington
A Friendship More Valuable Than Money

I was the first person Dayle Maloney signed up in network marketing in a company before Nutrition For Life. That company stopped paying checks and I told Dayle, "I'm done! I put all my energy into this company and I am not going to do it anymore."

He didn't argue with me — he knows I can be stubborn. Dayle just signed me up in Consumer Express (which was the company we call Nutrition For Life today). He didn't say a word; he just sent in my enrollment. I received the starter kit and totally ignored it. Dayle went ahead and ordered my first product.

Dayle knows I am stubborn — but not stupid. I decided, maybe I ought to look at this new company. He knew when I saw the quality of the product and the integrity of the company, I would build again. It was Dayle Maloney who kept me in network marketing. Dayle could just as easily have signed up a heavy-hitter and put that person in the first level position I have, but his loyalty to me and our friendship went beyond that.

I remember someone saying, "If you are in a large crowd of people and you want to find Dayle Maloney, look for the most condensed, compact group of people and he will be in the middle because people flock around him."

I discovered it works. While attending a large convention, I was looking for Dayle. I went to the balcony overlooking the ballroom and located the largest, thickest group of people; I saw a white head right in the middle. He is just like a magnet. Many of the top people in network marketing have a "standoffish" attitude, but with Dayle it has always been come one, come all.

Pat Johnson and Dayle Maloney
In 1981, before network marketing

Success Secret ...

"Dreams would never be achieved if people waited until all possible objections were overcome before they took action."

PART 6

Success In A Nutshell

Alane Roberts, Nutrition For Life, Manager, Account Management Department
The Makings Of A Network Marketing Giant

I have worked for Nutrition For Life since 1985 and during that time, I have met a good number of people.

Often in this industry, people reach a level of success and want certain special considerations and privileges. Their own self-gratification and egos are more important to them than courteous business practices or showing kindness towards others.

Dayle has never had that kind of an attitude. He has *never* been presumptuous about his position in the company. In the history of Nutrition For Life, Dayle has consistently been one of our most successful leaders.

We all know of achievers who, because of their success, treat others very poorly. Through the many years, the large amount of recognition and all the money, Dayle has stayed the same caring, loving, giving individual. Dayle Maloney's ability to cherish life and love the human race *more* with each added day — regardless if the day holds achievement or failure — is the measure of a truly successful person.

Dayle is one of our most consistent distributors. He keeps going even when he receives no recognition. I have a tremendous amount of respect for that. When he calls to check on a question, he doesn't expect to receive special favors. He lives by the same rules as everyone else in Nutrition For Life. In the office we give Dayle the same type of attention we would anyone else, and he is always very grateful for our efforts.

I have seen him receive many awards over the years, and every time he receives an award or recognition of any kind, he always says, "It is all because of my group and because of the help I have received."

One time, he was awarded a beautiful furniture set and said, "We should cut this furniture up into little pieces and share it with every person here because that is who it belongs to." He is very humble about his accomplishments and is always careful to give acknowledgement to those who have helped him.

If there was an example we could learn from Dayle, it would be that regardless of the challenges in our lives, people can succeed as Nutrition For Life distributors when they place their beliefs, dreams and hearts into their businesses.

The reason I have been at Nutrition For Life for over 13 years is my belief in the company, the program, and the quality of life I have witnessed people obtain by working the business. Nutrition For Life is dedicated to providing a realistic opportunity which people can use to better their lives. If I didn't believe it to be true, I couldn't work here.

A large number of the people in society talk big and never follow through with the actions. President David Bertrand, Executive Vice-President Jana Mitcham, and Dayle Maloney save the talk and instead walk the walk. I think that is a rare commodity in today's world.

PART 7

Attract Leaders By Improving Yourself

Art Meakin, 2-Star Platinum, Texas
Invest In Your Own Personal Development

My fiancée, Lauren Whittmore — a network marketing guru — and I have lived a MLM love affair since our first date. Lauren called me in October, 1994 and asked me out to a Dayle Maloney seminar. We loved it and have been successful in business and love ever since!

I entered the network marketing industry in July of 1975 and became a millionaire by age 37. My goal was to be a millionaire by age 35 — I missed it by two years. I retired for two years, spending most of my time at the beach. Boredom struck and I was enticed out of retirement March, 1994 to join Nutrition For Life because of Tom Schreiter and Dayle Maloney. Dayle is like "icing on the cake." The company is the cake, Dayle is the icing. He has a heart of gold.

If at Dayle's age, deep in debt and with his handicaps, he could make it in network marketing, anyone can. Dayle Maloney is proof nice guys do finish first.

To make success in network marketing a reality, training is imperative. When distributors first join and they are all excited, that's the most dangerous time. Without training, those unskilled distributors go out to sponsor people and fall flat on their faces. Then they quit and believe network marketing doesn't work.

To succeed, new distributors should build their businesses based on a two-year plan. The 1st six months are dedicated to training — the industry, the company, the products. They can sponsor people during this time, but their main focus is to be diligent students. The 2nd six months is the apprenticeship — working with their sponsors and their uplines to earn-while-they-learn by sponsoring a couple of people here and there.

With a strong belief in network marketing and the knowledge of what needs to be done to succeed, they graduate to being a mentor, a trainer, and a good sponsor to someone else. That's where they become leaders and earn at leadership levels.

To build a strong organization a person must be dedicated to becoming a really good sponsor, not just someone who recruits massive quantities of people and never helps them.

One of the main obligations in my organization is to retrain people — reset their expectations and perceptions on what network marketing is about — before they are sponsored into the business. We are in the training and development business with our prospects, not the hype and greed business. Over 90% of the network marketing companies are promoting their businesses and products on hype and greed. The results? People may join quickly, but they won't stick around because they enrolled for all the wrong reasons.

Never use hype and greed — use common sense. Provide your prospects with truthful information and let them decide if this opportunity works for them. If you pressure them in — they'll never do anything. If you have to hard-sell a person *once* to enroll them, you will have to *re-sell* them every week. That's counterproductive.

My Nutrition For Life organization has what is called the "safe ground rule" (a term I heard from one of my NFLI leaders, Michael Dlouhy). We stay on safe ground with our prospects and our distributors, never forcing them. We entice them by providing all the information they need. They make their own decisions.

We do give people incentives such as, "Join today and receive a free 6-hour training seminar," or "We will give you 100 free names and mailing pieces."

We won't pressure with the old line, "If you don't get in right now, you're really going to miss out." We don't do that, and I have to say I learned a portion of that from Dayle.

My philosophy is to get rich slowly rather than quickly. Be the tortoise rather than the hare because time-and-time again the tortoise wins the race. Dayle is the perfect example; he wasn't an overnight success, and $7,000,000.00 ago his first check was pretty small ($5.66).

Dayle does a great job summing up the financial reason for building a network marketing business. When someone asks, "How much did you make your first month?" Dayle says, "I don't know. I haven't finished collecting on it, yet."

Art Meakin and Lauren Whittmore

Success Secret ...

"The degree of success you experience in network marketing is directly related to the time you invest on personal development."

PART 8

Will This Improve Your Life?

Lee and Dee Dee Bryant
1-Star Platinum Executives, Minnesota
Creating An Emotional Response

If it weren't for Nutrition For Life both my wife, Dee Dee, and I agree she wouldn't be here today. In the late 1970's and early 1980's, Dee Dee was very sick. She was a patient at the famous Mayo Clinic six times in seven years. They said her illness was all in her head and there was nothing wrong with her.

A good friend of ours suggested that Dee Dee should go to a clinic in Nevada. We went and they discovered blockages on both sides of her neck, in her arms and legs. They suggested intravenous treatments that would take a month.

We did not plan on staying in Nevada for a month and Dee Dee doesn't like to be poked by a needle. We asked them if there was some other way we could do this. The doctor said, "Yes. You stay here and take as many of these intravenous treatments as you can. When you go home take Master Key Plus for 90 days (which is a Nutrition For Life product) and during that time work up to walking a mile a day. Then come back and we'll see what has happened."

We went home and Dee Dee was very conscientious about taking her Master Key and walking a mile a day. About 45 days into her home treatment, she came walking into the yard with a big smile: "Lee, I don't have to go back. I just walked three miles and I feel better than I did 20 years ago."

"Well, hey, we started something, let's finish it," I cautioned.

We went back and learned more. We became actively involved in alternative health care. I took correspondence courses where I researched and studied to become a naturopathic doctor. Nutrition For Life has totally changed our lives and given us freedom that most people can't understand. We go where we want, when we want, if we want and we stay as long as we want. I am on my fourth free car and Dee Dee has her second free motor home. This one is a $90,000 motor home that Nutrition for Life is paying for. If you had that, would that change your life? Yes. Amen.

Lee and Dee Dee Bryant,
1-Star Platinum Executives, Minnesota

PART 9

Winning Friends and Influencing People

Angie Gustafsson, Platinum Executive, California
It Is Nice To Be Important,
But It Is More Important To Be Nice

The sweetest word to people's ears is THEIR NAME — it makes people feel important and accepted when they are *known* by others. A number of successful people, especially speakers, forget the "little people" who got them there.

Dayle meets hundreds of people and remembers their names; it's amazing. Exhausted, he will shake hands, talk to people and take photos until everyone has left. He always eats his meals with everyone to give others a chance to spend time with him.

I see so many leaders who, once they develop some amount of recognition, become tired of talking to people who may never be "successful" in that leader's eyes. Those leaders lose interest in the little person who is struggling. Dayle thinks and acts just the opposite. He doesn't judge anyone based on their current life situation. He gives everyone individual attention and never turns down the opportunity to shake a hand.

It was a dream of mine to speak in front of thousands of people and have something important to share. I searched for occasions to speak, and during that time I became excited about the Nutrition For Life business opportunity. Incredible health turnarounds happened in my family using the products, and I began to share this information with people through free 30-minute product meetings.

Dayle approached me and said, "I heard you've been holding product meetings. How would you like to offer them all across the country?"

I could hardly believe my ears. My heart went crazy, and I replied, "Are you kidding? I would love to!"

Dayle put me on the road and has kept me there ever since. It's a thrill making a living doing what I love — amazingly the money just follows. If I hadn't kept believing and dreaming that someday I would be a speaker, if I had let that dream die, I would probably be in a dead-end career dreading each day.

You must keep your dream alive and go for it. Take action to achieve your dreams, and when you do, incredible doors open — like the phone call out of the blue from Dayle. I presented free seminars for 18 months — and eventually someone, who could open a door for me, found out and enhanced the quality of my entire life.

Angie and Fred Gustafsson, California

Success Secret ...

"A leader who develops *people* adds to
their organization; a leader who
develops *leaders* multiplies their
organization."

PART 10

The Single Most Powerful Secret Of Success

Skeeter Trahan, Manager, Order Department,
Nutrition For Life,
People Do Not Follow Programs,
They Follow Leaders Who Inspire Them

In 1985, I went to work in Lake Charles, Louisiana for Consumer Express which became Nutrition For Life. Later, I relocated to Houston when the company moved. I've known David Bertrand and Jana Mitcham since I was 17 and started working for the company. I know David's family extremely well since I went to school with his two children. Our families were both members of the same church in Louisiana.

I first met Dayle in 1985. He was visiting the company headquarters and I helped carry books out to his vehicle. Because of Dayle's accomplishments, I had expectations of a giant of a business person. When we met, I saw a tender man who walked with a limp.

Dayle talked to me and was interested in me. As we were loading Dayle's vehicle, I couldn't understand how this man — who had all of this going for him — could be genuinely interested in such a little person as myself. I was 17 and just a kid.

My first impression of Dayle was that "Here is a man who actually cares enough to talk to me!" He has consistently shown the same interest over and over during the last 13 years. Dayle cares about the individual and the "small" person. It doesn't matter how much business you are going to bring to him, Dayle encourages the "little" people to be "big" people in a way that works for them.

He displays every fruit of God's Spirit: love, joy, peace, longsuffering, kindness, goodness, faithfulness, gentleness, self-control. Dayle has accomplished much success and is not arrogant but rather very humble. I could compare him to the pastor of a church. Dayle has an incredible pastor's heart and shepherds over his group and other groups. He is not isolated to just the people in his own downline; he cares about everyone.

He knows my wife and kids. There are not many people who are as famous and well-connected as Dayle who would take the time to know everything about me. He is leaving an incredible legacy. When he is gone, Dayle will have left so much good behind — the people whose hearts he has touched, the people who love him. I've watched Dayle for 13 years live a life where he consistently leads by example. He walks what he talks, and talks what he walks.

Success Secret ...

"Love and respect are not automatically given to a leader. They must be earned."

Nutrition For Life Distributor Spotlight ...

Fred Kalkofen, Gold Executive, Wisconsin

"Dayle Maloney makes people feel good about themselves. They enjoy the time they spend with him, don't want to leave and look forward to seeing him again."

— **Fred Kalkofen, Gold Executive, Wisconsin**

PART 11

Finishing First

Greg Pusey, Board of Directors, Nutrition For Life International
"Can Good People Really Finish First?"

Dayle's money did not come because he wanted to get rich. Instead, Dayle pursued *the dream* — what he perceived to be a good opportunity to help other people. From that desire to teach and motivate, using network marketing as the vehicle, Dayle made himself a good living. He loves what he does because he loves to see people get ahead.

For Dayle, business is not about what he can take from others. In fact, he has been criticized by people because he often sells his tapes and books at prices so low he makes no money on his business building tools. Dayle wants the information in your hands so you can get ahead. He's not looking to make money off you while you are trying to get ahead.

Dayle teaches people about success, goal setting, and striving to achieve: "If you get kicked and you are down ... don't let it keep you down." Dayle shows people how to move from "I cannot" to "I can." He causes people to believe they can really accomplish what they desire. Dayle is a person who marches with vision. He hangs on to that vision, and he just keeps working and working until he gets to where he wants to be.

He lights up a room with his down-home wisdom and humor causing his audiences to feel close to him because Dayle is a real person. Yes, Dayle Maloney is living proof that with persistence good folks do finish first — both in friendships and fortunes.

Success Secret ...

"When you take your eyes off yourself and put them on others, your business will grow."

PART 12

Keeping Your
Reputation Clean

Don't you dare tarnish your reputation with a company that's not going to be around. When you go out and tell someone about Nutrition for Life — it's not my reputation on the line — it's yours.

You have to make sure the company you represent is going to be around. In my first network marketing company I personally enrolled over 2,000 people and the company quit writing bonus checks.

Let me tell you how bad it can get. I had two serious death threats on my life from people in my downline. I was informed by the Detroit Police Department not to come into Detroit for a seminar I had scheduled because they knew the guy threatening me. I didn't even sponsor him. Someone I sponsored, sponsored him. But he blamed me and I had nothing to do with the company going out of business!

You have to find a long-term opportunity. How easy is it to do? Ninety percent of network marketing companies never see their second birthday, and 95% of them never see their fifth birthday.

In 1986, Jeannine and I were featured on the cover of a network marketing magazine in an article called, "Portrait of a Winner." I picked the magazine up again about 6 months ago and there were 67 network marketing programs advertised. Only four of those are still in business today — four out of 67! I am proud to tell you, one of them was Nutrition For Life International.

You have picked the right company — Nutrition For Life will be here for generations to come. If you are a distributor in Nutrition For Life and you don't put the pedal to the medal, you and I will never know how many people's lives you could be touching.

And if you don't get involved, you and I will never know how many lives you could be touching in the years to come. It could be a few. It could be a handful. It could be thousands of lives around the world that you could be helping with better health and wealth.

Nutrition For Life is the opportunity of a lifetime. Up until now, you've most likely never seen an opportunity like this. And you'll probably never see another one like it for the rest of your life. Take action now. Why? Remember, opportunities are never lost, they are simply found by someone else.

Success Secret ...

"You only have a future if the company has a future. If the company goes out of business — so do you. When the company stops writing checks — so do you."

**Jeannine's Lexus and my Lexus are both paid for by
Nutrition For Life.**

**Just 15 years ago, I couldn't afford a $425 a month rent
payment. This is the lakeside home in Wisconsin where
Jeannine and I live.**

The view of the lake off my patio. I love it.

I'm out on the patio with my boys, Benny and Barney.
They're looking on anxiously as I feed Tara's little one.

Jeannine and me on stage at the Nutrition For Life National Convention in Minneapolis.

Here is Dayle Maloney's Latest Project...

Karing for Kids

Dayle Maloney wants to open the Dawson McAllister HopeLine 24 hrs a day, 7 days a week, 365 days a year and he needs your help ...

Dear Friend:

HopeLine is a "let's talk" hotline for kids 21 years and younger. What do they talk about?

"I don't know what my problem is. I come from a 'perfect family.' I am anorexic and so ugly. I don't trust myself and sometimes I just want to die. Help me!"

"I ran away last year. I did a lot of drugs and drinking. I feel horribly depressed and suicidal. Help!"

These are excerpts from actual calls for help and they break my heart. Is there hope for these kids? Is it too late — ? Last year for the 64,000 callers who received help, at least *that many* went unanswered. Why? HopeLine's current funding allows the toll-free call line to be open only 6 ½ hours a day — and many kids aren't even aware it exists.

Last year the volunteers at the Dawson McAllister HopeLine operated on a shoe string budget with single line phones, pads of paper and pencils. Imagine receiving over 248,000 calls since 1992 over a few phone lines with no computer system to generate ongoing logs. When kids call in they have the frustration of starting all over from the beginning with a new volunteer.

The HopeLine could be helping more kids right now ... if they just had the money. How much longer can we remain indifferent to these kids — how many lives can we afford to throw away?

I need your help. I've committed to raising $1,000,000 this year to open HopeLine 24 hours a day/7 days week/365days a year ... for the kids. Please join me by filling out the reply card below. Let your contribution be as large as your faith, and as heartfelt as your prayers ... Let's work together to remove pain and suffering from today's youth ...

_ _ _ _ _ _ Cut out along this line and return to address below _ _ _ _ _ _ _ _.

____ **Yes, Dayle!** I want to help you open the HopeLine 24 hours a day, 7 days a week, 365 days a year. I realize the average expense per kid's call into the toll-free HopeLine is $5.00. I am helping with a monthly or one time contribution as indicated below.

____ Yes! Dayle, I want to help you and the HopeLine *every month*.

___ $250 ___$100 ___$50 ___$25 ___ other _____

Visa/MC _____ Exp _____

signature_____

____ Yes, Dayle, I want to help you and HopeLine with a *one time* contribution.

___$1,000 ___ $500 ___ $250 ___ $100 ___other _____

Visa/MC _____ Exp _____

signature_____

Please make checks payable and send this form to:
Dawson McAllister HopeLine
PO Box 26746, Benbrook, Texas 76126
or call your contribution into the HopeLine at 931-388-9635

- -

Listen to the Dawson McAllister Live! radio show on over 268 Christian stations, Sundays from 7 p.m. to 9 p.m., central time.

They are a 501(c)(3) federally tax exempt organization, all contributions tax deductible to the full extent of the law.

The Best Of Dayle Maloney

8 cassette tapes in a beautiful album

Learn From The Legend Himself!

"If you could take down 1/10 of what Dayle Maloney says and put it to use, you'd be a certain success."
— Tom "Big Al" Schreiter, World Famous Network Marketing Author

"Dayle Maloney, in my opinion, is one of the small handful of extraordinary achievers in the network marketing industry. He is a doer, not a talker … and when he talks, everybody should listen." — David Bertrand, President NFLI

Enjoy more secrets and techniques for success in life and business. This audio album contains 6 live convention and rally recordings plus 2 training seminars.

Now Just $29.95

If You Aren't Plugged In … You Can't Get Turned On!

4 cassette tapes in a handsome album

"It is Dayle's passion that sets him apart — his passion for establishing genuine relationships with people. His ultimate goal is to help everyone become successful in network marketing."
— Jana Mitcham, Executive Vice-President Nutrition For Life

Sizzle Topics include: Who to and how to sponsor as executives, how to increase your bonus check, how to get rich, how to achieve platinum, 3 keys to explosive growth, simple sponsoring plus much, much more!

Now just $29.95

TO ORDER TAPES

Please send me the following items:

Quantity	Title	Unit Price	Total
_____	_____	_____	_____
_____	_____	_____	_____
_____	_____	_____	_____

Subtotal	_____
5% sales tax (WI only)	_____
Shipping and Handling	$ 5.00
Total Order	_____

By Telephone: MC, VISA, American Express or Discover call 800-451-6588 or 1-800-621-2065.

By Mail: Just fill out the information below and send with your remittance to:

Dayle Maloney & Associates
3301 Golf Road
Eau Claire, WI 54701

Name _____

Address _____

City _____ State _____ Zip _____

Visa/MasterCard Am. Ex./ Discover _____ Exp. _____

Signature _____

Check enclosed for $ _____ payable to Dayle Maloney

Daytime Telephone (   )_____

Home Telephone (   ) _____